How to Shop for Free

HOW TO

Shop *for* *Free*

Shopping Secrets for Smart Women
Who Love to Get Something for Nothing

Kathy Spencer
with Samantha Rose

Da Capo
∞
LIFE
LONG
A Member of the Perseus Books Group

Design and production by Eclipse Publishing Services
Set in 10.5-point Adobe Caslon

Cataloging-in-Publication data for this book is available from the Library of Congress.

First Da Capo Press edition 2010
ISBN: 978-0-7382-1456-6
Library of Congress Control Number: 2010935518

Published by Da Capo Press
A Member of the Perseus Books Group
www.dacapopress.com

Da Capo Press books are available at special discounts for bulk purchases in the U.S. by corporations, institutions, and other organizations. For more information, please contact the Special Markets Department at the Perseus Books Group, 2300 Chestnut Street, Suite 200, Philadelphia, PA, 19103, or call (800) 810-4145, ext. 5000, or e-mail special.markets@perseusbooks.com.

10 9 8 7 6 5 4 3 2 1

*Dedicated to my husband Brian
and my children Crystal, Kelsie, Chance, and Parker*

*And for my "other" family,
all the How to Shop for Free members*

Contents

Introduction

Have you ever entered a promotional code on a website that you frequent, used a gift certificate, cashed in on "award" dollars, or shopped at a sample sale? If so, you've already done half of what you need to do in order to shop for free. The other half is what I know and what I'm about to teach you.

Who am I? I'm just a regular mom. I live in a nice suburban neighborhood on the East Coast. I drive the kind of SUV you see on the road every day, and I dress my kids in many of the same clothes your kids may ask for. But, what's different about me is that the majority of my expenses are, amazingly, free. So amazing in fact, that over the past year I've captured the attention of millions of American women, eager for me to show them how to get the ultimate deal— 100 percent off your total sale.

Get this: I've managed to get a $267.22 grocery bill down to one cent. That's right—one penny. At a time when it's tough to make ends meet, I've figured out how to shop for free. *Don't believe me?*

Most people are incredulous when I tell them that I can get something for nothing, but it's true. I get a lot for nothing. I have four kids ages eighteen to four; we have a dog, three cats, and a bunny, and in an average week, I spend under $4 on two to three carts full of groceries, including fresh meat and seafood, fruits and vegetables, canned goods, toilet paper, laundry detergent, and pet food. In fact, I can gloat that I've been known to make money after shopping and still take home that much loot. As you can imagine, women who love a good bargain want to know: What's your secret?

I'll tell you what I've told them: I've cracked the code. Legally, of course; I play by the rules. I've simply created a strategic way to shop that maximizes promotions and sales to save thousands of dollars a year. Right now, my three-story house is stocked with goods I've gotten totally for free. And here's the best part: it's easy and, dare I say, fun (and in this economy, pretty darn cool). Once you get the hang of it, you'll be surprised by the items on your shopping list that you'll never need to buy again. Things like: toothpaste, tampons, and Tabasco. Trust me, shopping for free is addictive.

Every day on my website, www.howtoshopforfree.net, a mob of women (and a growing number of men) visit to learn the basics of how to spend less and get more for themselves and their families. And while I regularly write articles, share my tips, and often meet groups of other east coast sales addicts to shop alongside me, what members haven't gotten is my overall program: a step-by-step shopping guide for busy women on a budget who want to pay next to nothing and score the kind of deals that make you feel like you've gotten away with something. That's where this book comes in.

Throughout the next twelve chapters, I will teach you something financial guru Suze Orman hasn't—how, with a five dollar bill and a new approach to shopping, you can buy groceries, household items, even cosmetics and clothes, and have money left over. You do the math— that's not just slashing your bill in half. That's getting it for nothing.

Hold up. Am I a "Coupon Lady"? No more than you are if you answered "yes" to any of the questions in the first paragraph. The fact is that nearly every American woman uses some form of promotion or "coupon" in one way or another to get more for less. So as far as I'm concerned, you and I are just the same. The only difference is that I've figured out how to really work it to get even more—and I can show you how to do it, too.

Truthfully, I never meant to make a name for myself as a consumer spending bad@ss . I'm just like many women I know, looking for ways to ease financial stress for our families in tough economic times and still live like we want to. But since I cracked the coupon code and started showing my friends and family how they, too, could shop for free, I haven't had a spare moment. Between the demands of my online community, my own family, and all the media knocking on my door, I can hardly get to my own shopping list, which is why I've decided to put what I know into one concise guidebook that teaches anyone who wants to save money just how to do it. If you're a single gal who would love to cut your expenses on the boring stuff like kitty litter and plastic wrap so you can still afford the better things in life, I'll show you how. Or if you're a mother like me, I'll show you how to slash your monthly spending and budget for the big stuff, like a remodeled kitchen, a new car paid for with cash, and your kids' college tuition.

In the pages that follow, you'll learn how to find the best savings and combine them with store promotions, awards programs, and store credit to get the following items for free:

- Meat and veggies
- Packaged and frozen foods
- Beer and wine
- Makeup, shampoo, and hair color
- Toothpaste, toilet paper, and paper towels
- Baby wipes and diapers
- Greeting cards and wrapping paper

- Cold medicine and prescription drugs
- Curtains, pillows, and linens
- Cleaning supplies
- School supplies
- Brand-name clothing
- and even fill up at the gas station!

And there's more even beyond this book. Be sure to check out www.howtoshopforfree.net for up-to-date savings, suggestions, and tips from yours truly as well as other bargainistas (and bargainistos— yep, men shop for free, too).

If I have my way, you'll never pay top retail dollar on the basic, and not-so-basic, stuff again. Additionally, you won't ever run out of the essentials. Before learning how to shop for free, a San Francisco urbanite confessed to me that once after using her last roll of toilet paper without realizing it, in a moment of "uh-oh" panic, she resorted to paper coffee filters as a substitute. I promise that with a little shopping strategy and pre-planning, this won't ever happen to you. In fact, I hope to teach you how to get so far ahead of the shopping game that you're in a position to give stuff away to others who need it. Furthermore, throughout these pages, I aim to change your perception of what it means to "clip," steer you away from fake deals, and reveal every shopping secret I know. Follow the steps in the pages ahead and by the end of the book, you will have more of what you want for less.

1

How to Shop for Free, A–Z

First, let's start with a shift in thinking. Shopping for free begins with how you approach the shopping experience, and so I'm just going to come out and say it: Lazy shoppers don't shop for free. You know who I mean—the woman who is resigned to paying full retail prices because she wants it when she wants it. We all love convenience, but I'll be honest; you're never going to find that $120 pair of skinny jeans for $2.99 until you give up some amount of accommodation for the reward. Shopping for free requires some upfront planning, strategizing, and dusting off your basic addition and subtraction skills. *Don't freak out.* Once you get the hang of it, shopping for free will just become a habit—one that'll make you feel like you're beating the system every time you walk out of a store.

What most women don't know is that when you put your savvy, smarts, and strategic mind to work, it's not about *finding* deals, but about *making* deals happen for you every time you shop. I shop deliberately and competitively. For me, shopping for free is an extreme sport, and my goal is to win. Why else would I play?

Do you think you don't have time to take your shopping game up a notch? Do you think that following sales is more trouble than it's worth? I admit, I've been criticized for having too much free time to do what I do, implying that the average woman doesn't have any extra hours to "work" at shopping. I have a husband, four kids, and a house full of pets. Believe me, I'm not sitting around thumbing through magazines while my nails dry. I do, however, set aside several hours a week to collect online coupons, scan circulars, and hit the stores. To me, this is time well spent considering, on average, I spend twenty dollars a month on groceries. That's right—twenty bucks! I bet that's less than you paid for your last manicure.

I'm not going to lie—shopping for free takes effort, but it doesn't mean you have to drastically change your lifestyle or use your hard-earned vacation days to shop for groceries. You just have to be willing to make a little extra time to change your shopping habits. You've already begun to do that by picking up this book. So keep reading. I'll make it worth your while.

What's in the cart?

Here's what you'll find in this chapter:
- The basics of *How to Shop for Free*
- Where to find the best savings
- The difference between "clipping" and "printing"
- And the best way to tap into the online and social media coupon craze

Get into the Game

Okay, now that your head is in the game, let's begin to answer some of your more pressing questions, like, Do I *really* have to use coupons? The answer is no, of course you can do whatever you wish, but if you want to score the best deals and live with less debt, I'd strongly suggest getting over any lingering coupon phobias. Perhaps I need to take a minute here to assure you that using coupons does not make you elderly or cheap. I'm certain you picked up this book knowing better, but old stereotypes are hard to shake. Let me give you a little background, including the latest statistics on coupon use.

The coupon is no stranger to American culture. It first appeared in 1894, when Asa Candler bought the formula for Coca-Cola and distributed hand-written tickets for a free glass of his new fountain drink. The coupon rose in popularity during the Great Depression and became a staple in American households throughout the '50s and '60s, peaking in the early '90s when a record 7.9 billion of them were redeemed in a single year (that's a lot of free stuff, people).

But then coupon use saw a slow decline. The practice fell out of fashion and became passé. It got categorized as something only those on a fixed income would do. Until 2009, when the coupon made an impressive comeback. One might say that the recession brought the sexy back to coupons. For the first time since 1992, consumers began redeeming coupons en masse. According to Inmar, a coupon-processing firm, businesses issued 367 billion coupons in 2009, and consumers redeemed 3.5 billion—a meteoric rise in usage that constituted a "new trend." As further evidence of the resurgence of coupon usage, Inmar reported that consumers "clipped" 92% more online coupons, and Yahoo reported that coupons ranked first on its list of economy-related searches in 2009. Biggies like the *New York Times*, the *Wall Street Journal*, and the *Chicago Tribune* reported that coupons, along with layaway programs and early bird dinners (cleverly renamed "twilight dining") are attracting a younger, hipper generation of women, couples, and urban hipsters who have decided that saving money and still getting what they want in hard times is cool.

And if I do say so, I fall right into this category—well, the hip one, anyway. I don't look like the stereotypical coupon clipper and neither do the rest of my newly forty friends—I'm thin, fit, and fashionable. My husband calls me his "Golden Ticket," not his Golden Girl.

So, now that you can rest assured that the young, hip, and hot are taking advantage of coupons to stretch their hard-earned dollars, let's tackle this idea that using coupons means you're miserly, tight, or a cheapskate. Saving money means you're smart. I eat better, dress nicer, and live more comfortably than most people I know because I've figured out how to strategically use coupons to get more of what I want for less.

From this page forward, I want you to start thinking of those little squares of paper with the barcodes on them as cash. Personally, I can't look at them any other way because using them has saved me, on average, over $60,000 a year. That's a decent yearly salary, wouldn't you agree? I'd be an idiot not to use them, and I think you can see where I'm going with this. Saving money is chic, so get that warped image out of your head of you, the penny-pincher, hobbling down the aisles with your shopping basket and change purse. That's just not you. And it's definitely not me.

There's one more thing I need to mention before we get started. In case you're feeling a little criminal, like what you're about to read is a "how-to" on cheating the system, let me assure you that's not the case. I play by the rules, and I hope you will, too. The truth is that when customers use coupons, the stores get fully reimbursed by the manufacturer. Plus, stores get incentives for using coupons to bring in new business and push specific products. They're in it to win it, so there's nothing for you to feel guilty about. Even when you get the ultimate deal— 100% off your total sale—the stores and the manufacturer score, too.

The Basics:
Store Versus Manufacturer Coupons

I'm guessing most of you are *How to Shop for Free* newbies who probably never imagined picking up a coupon book. For most people, the grocery bill is their biggest weekly expense, so I think it's the perfect place to start. I'll teach you how to shop for sexier items later on, I promise, but for now, let's start with the essentials. There are two basic types of coupons: manufacturer coupons and store coupons.

Manufacturer Coupons

Product manufacturers—including giants in the marketplace like Procter & Gamble, Kraft, Betty Crocker, General Mills, and Kellogg's—regularly issue coupons that you can redeem in stores where their products are sold. Manufacturer coupons usually don't expire for two to three months so using them right away isn't necessary. In fact, it's more strategic for you to put them aside for a later date when you can combine them with a store coupon for significant savings. Yes, you can combine coupons! That's what Chapter 3: Woo Hoo Deal Alert is all about, so stick around. A manufacturer coupon will say "manufacturer" or "MFR" coupon at the top. MFR is coupon-speak and is only one of many couponisms you'll encounter throughout these pages. Introducing you to a new subculture with its own dialect will challenge you, but I'm going to do it anyway. I'd be cheating you out of a proper *How to Shop for Free* education if I didn't provide you with the latest shopper-slang. How, or if, you use it is up to you.

The most dependable place to find **manufacturer coupons** is in your local Sunday newspaper. They're in that bundle of colorful, glossy inserts jammed into the middle of the paper. That's your cash allowance for the week, so don't throw it away. Repeat after me: "I don't throw away coupons because coupons are like cash and that would be stupid." Sunday coupon inserts are distributed by coupon companies SmartSource (SS) and RedPlum (RP) and manufacturers like Procter & Gamble (PG) and General Mills (GM). The Sunday inserts contain coupons for a wide variety of products ranging from shaving cream to popcorn to fiber-rich yogurt. There will be products throughout these inserts you'll swear you'd *never* spend money on, stick in your mouth, or stash in your bathroom. I'm fairly certain I'll change your mind on this later on, but for now, go ahead and hold on to your

HOT TIP: Be Unconventional

Shopping for free requires upfront planning and, sometimes, unconventional methods. In Chapter 2: Get It Together and Make a Plan, I'll explain exactly why it's important to get your hands on as many Sunday inserts as you can. For now, just know it's one of my favorite *How to Shop for Free* strategies, and here are a few ways to go about it.

Start a Paper Route: On Sunday night or Monday morning, most gas station/convenience stores will let you remove the coupon inserts from any unsold Sunday newspapers before they're picked up Monday morning and returned to the distributor—in my case, the *Boston Globe*. A friend of mine does this every Monday morning and refers to it as her "paper route."

Take a Dive: You can also find coupon inserts at recycling centers where discarded newspapers arrive daily. This might seem a little desperado to some of you; granted, it is a form of dumpster diving. If scavenging is going too far for you, try asking your friends and neighbors for their discarded Sunday inserts. Most people will be happy to hand them over. I even know a woman who's taken up a coupon collection at her church, bless her heart.

Pay a Dollar: Many dollar stores sell the Sunday paper for a dollar. Get four papers for the price of one!

conviction that tilapia fish sticks and hemorrhoid cream will never make it into your shopping cart. Just do me one favor: Don't throw any coupons away.

Local Weeklies: Not someone who gets the Sunday paper? No biggie. Try your local weeklies. A lot of regional papers, many of which are free, include coupon inserts. I've found a smaller suburban paper that puts the previous week's Smart-Source inserts in their Thursday edition. It's only fifty cents, so I can buy four or five and walk away with a nice stash of coupons for the price of one Sunday *Globe*. Better yet, I've found a local free paper that comes out every Friday that includes the upcoming Sunday SmartSource inserts. I call these "coupons from the future," and, appropriately, I feel totally ahead of the game when I score a stack of these. I've also discovered that some Saturday editions of large metro newspapers contain coupon inserts. Start sniffing around and see what's available in your area.

Click and Print: Not someone who wants to mess with newspapers at all? That's not a deal breaker because coupons aren't only found in newspaper inserts. You can continue to just throw them out with the recycling if you like, but you'll be throwing out a potential gold mine. (I'm wincing just thinking about it.) They're online, too, for those of you who would rather print or "key" than clip, and I'll go deeply into the online coupon craze a bit later in the chapter.

Store Coupons

Store coupons look just like MFR coupons, but they say something store-specific like "redeemable only at Whole Foods Market" or "Target Coupon." They are issued by individual stores and redeemable *only* in that store. You'll find store coupons in your local newspapers (store circulars usually come out mid-week), in the stores themselves, and on the store's website. Store coupons have a much shorter shelf life than MFR coupons because they tend to correspond to a current store sale or promotion, and, typically, the sale and the coupons expire within a week to ten days.

Additional Hidden Savings

Let's say you're already hip to Sunday inserts and store circulars and you're thinking, *Tell me something I don't already know.* Okay, smarty pants, here goes. Let's talk about the hidden savings that exist throughout the stores where you currently shop. It's not that your stores don't want you to find these savings, but rather you haven't yet trained your eye to spot them. Once you do that, you'll notice them everywhere.

When I enter a store, I immediately get into my shopper stance: knees slightly bent, core tight, hands free, and my attention focused. (I wasn't kidding when I said that for me, shopping is an extreme sport.) The first thing I do before heading into the aisles to shop is hit the rack of weekly store circulars, which is usually located in the front of the store. Often, you'll find additional loose coupons and coupon booklets there. When I do, I snatch 'em right up. Then, I cruise over to the service desk and ask if the folks there have any store coupons. Most stores regularly print out their weekly coupons and have stacks of them behind the desk. All you have to do is ask for them.

As I shop up and down the aisles, I look for **peelies** (yep, more lingo), coupons that are attached to products that you "peel" off, and that's exactly what I do. Don't be fooled: You don't need to buy the product to get the peelie. Additionally, I look for **tear pads,** pads of MFR coupons within the store, and **blinkies,** those red electronic machines in the grocery aisles that "blink" and spit out coupons. Along the way, I look for any product displays. Nine times out of ten, there's a tear pad attached to it.

After I pay for my groceries and head to the car, I check my store receipt. Often, it will include a coupon for something I just bought that I can use during my next shopping trip.

Chances are you've never noticed these hidden savings before, or if you have, you probably haven't given them much attention. Well, that was the old, naive you. Your favorite stores offer you many additional ways to save, so the next time you walk through their doors, get into your shopper stance and start snatching up savings.

You Asked It

Q: *Should I immediately clip the coupons I know I'm going to use and put the others aside? (Notice that my bargainistas know better than to say, "and throw the rest away?")*

A: *If it's a store coupon, yes. Clip it right away because if you're going to use it, you'll probably need to do so within the week. If it's an MFR coupon, there are a couple schools of thought on this. Some shoppers like to clip the coupons right away for the products they can imagine needing in the next couple of months. (Remember: MFR coupons are typically good for two to three months.) While there's nothing wrong with this method, I go about it differently. I choose to leave my Sunday inserts intact and file them away by the date they came out. If you look very closely at the spine of the insert (for those of you who are far-sighted, you might need a magnifying glass), you'll notice an itty-bitty date. I write this date on the front of my inserts in a thick, black marker and put them aside until I'm ready to use them. Also, because I collect multiple inserts (multiple coupons = more free stuff), keeping my inserts intact, versus trying to manage a mess of tiny paper cut-outs, is the best way I've found to stay organized. Trust me—organization is key if you want to shop for free.*

In Chapter 2: Get It Together and Make a Plan, I'll go deeper into my filing system and give you lots of ideas on how to organize your personal savings stash. So, if you're one of those single-drawer-as-filing-system people, don't worry about it. Stash all your coupons in one drawer/folder/envelope for now, and I'll help you streamline your mess later.

To Clip or to Print

While clipping coupons out of the Sunday newspaper is still the most common way people get their coupons (an average of 100–300 are distributed this way each week), the digital coupon craze is exploding right before my very eyes, and one of the reasons for this is that many shoppers (and perhaps you, too) want to do all their "clipping" online. In response to the online trend, coupon distributors like SmartSource and RedPlum have made this totally possible. If you don't get your hands on the Sunday newspaper inserts, you can easily find many of the same coupons online and print them at home. What's more, you can select to print only those coupons you absolutely want.

SmartSource

Go directly to www.coupons.smartsource.com for a complete listing of printable grocery coupons. The online deals tend to be a little bit different from what's in the Sunday inserts but not by much. Plus, if you sign up to become a member, you'll receive their *New Deal Alerts* via e-mail every day.

RedPlum

Go to www.redplum.com for RedPlum's exclusive grocery coupons. Online members also have access to RedPlum's Secret Sales for popular retailers like Best Buy, Old Navy, and Barnes and Noble.

Procter & Gamble

If you miss out on the P&G Saver Solutions booklet delivered in the Sunday paper, go to www.pgesaver.com where you can load Procter & Gamble coupons directly onto your store loyalty card (more on this fancy technology later). Members of the site also qualify for additional P&G coupons and free product samples that will be sent directly to your home.

Coupons.com

In addition to the three sites just mentioned, www.coupons.com is a fabulous resource for grocery printables. This site also gives you the option of loading savings directly onto your store card and offers discount codes for many popular online shopping destinations like Victoria's Secret, Expedia, Amazon, and Babies R Us.

Once you start cruising around online (just for fun try googling "printable coupon"), I think you'll be happy, and maybe even a bit over-whelmed, to discover that most paper coupons have a corresponding online version. So if collecting stacks of paper inserts isn't your thing, find your favorite deals online and start printing. *A word of warning:* Some stores have stopped taking printable coupons due to an increase in coupon fraud (i.e., losers creating their own fake deals). Check your store's policy online or ask a cashier the next time you shop whether or not they accept printables before you waste valuable printer ink and paper.

HOT TIP: Use the Back Button

We may play by the rules, but that doesn't mean we ignore a cool insider's trick when we stumble across one. After a coupon prints, sometimes (but not always) if you hit the backspace bar on your browser, an identical coupon will spit out of your printer—just like that. I've been known to consistently get two of the same coupon this way. Give it a try.

Also, printable coupons reset themselves the first of the month. So, if you've printed the maximum number of coupons the site will allow on, say, the 28th, you can print them again on the first of the month. Score.   ✂

Printer Alert

I think it goes without saying that you need a printer to print coupons. Before you're able to print, however, most coupon sites like smart-source.com will warn you: "You may be prompted to download a small, free software application in order to print your coupons." Whether you like it or not, until someone comes up with a speedier alternative, you'll have to download this Java application in order to print. Installing the application allows you to print high-resolution barcodes that a retailer can scan (no scan, no deal), and it controls the number of coupons that can be printed in order to prevent fraud and protect the manufacturer. And because we are women who play by the rules, we should respect our retailers on this one. Of course you can refuse, but if you ask me, it's a harmless program that takes up little to no space on your hard drive, so go ahead and do it. If you're worried about viruses, spyware, or adware then read the fine print. Most sites will assure you the application is safe.

The Downside to Printing

Printing coupons is quick, convenient, and maybe more contemporary than clipping the old-fashioned way, but there are only so many coupons one woman can get her hands on by printing from her home computer alone. In Chapter 3: Woo Hoo Deal Alert, I'll explain why, when shopping for free, it's a good idea to get coupons from a variety of sources. Until then, consider scoring more "printable" coupons in the following ways:

- Print from the office and ask your colleagues (the ones who owe you favors) to also print for you.
- Ask your girlfriends (until they catch on to how much stuff you're getting for free and want in on the action) to print for you.
- Bribe your teenagers with food/money/whatever it takes to print coupons for you at school—not during class, of course!

The Online and Social Media Coupon Craze

Okay, so maybe you want to get away from paper all together. For those of you who want to go totally green and like the convenience of shopping online, here are some great digital options.

E-Coupons

I mentioned before that on the Procter & Gamble website and at coupons.com, users are invited to put savings directly onto their store loyalty cards. You bypass the cutting and printing process altogether by electronically loading coupons onto your store swipe card.

How it works: Sign up as a member on the site. Once you create a password and log onto the site, start browsing for coupons you want to load onto your savings card. You'll be asked what store you want to "ADD" your online coupons to and then you'll be asked to register your store savings card number. As soon as you input your information, your online coupons magically appear on your savings card. It's that easy.

To redeem your e-coupon savings, you simply hand your "loaded" card to the cashier at checkout, and the dollars are automatically deducted from your total bill. Super simple! What coupons you don't use, stay on your card until you use them or they expire. Most of the grocery store chains have made, or are making, this available to customers. Check your stores' websites to see what they offer.

Sites like Shortcuts and Cellfire (see Resources for URLs) have streamlined the e-coupon process for you. It's like one-stop shopping. Sign up for the online service and load deals from a number of stores directly onto your loyalty cards from one central site. This saves you time. Participating stores include Vons, Safeway, Randall's, Kroger, Smith's, Ralph's Hilander, and Dominick's. And if that doesn't make it easy for the online crowd to shop for free, Cellfire can also send coupons directly to your mobile phone that you scan at the register.

Mobile Coupons

Mobile coupons are typically text messages or e-mail alerts that a retailer or manufacturer sends directly to your cell phone. Target (which has a special place in my heart) was one of the first national retailers to make mobile coupons available to its customers. The text message will include either a barcode or a promotional number code that you show to the cashier for scanning. No cutting. No printing. No paper at all. Just be sure your cell phone battery is charged before you get in the check-out line.

Mobile coupons offer a range of savings from the basics like groceries and cleaning supplies to more indulgent "gets" like spa services, happy-hour deals, theater tickets, and pet grooming. Tons of individual retailers are getting into this game. In fact, I'm sure that as

I'm writing this, more mobile opportunities are becoming available. Check the Resources section at the end of the chapter for some of the more popular mobile coupon apps.

Savings with Social Media

No doubt, you're beginning to realize that potential savings are everywhere. And while I don't want to overwhelm you (it's only Chapter 1), I do want to discuss how to shop for free using social media. The truth is, the insider's scoop on many of the best deals is found on Twitter, Facebook, and all over the blogosphere.

Twitter

Hard-core shoppers who are technically savvy (this group soon to include you) are using Twitter to spread the word about bad@ss bargains. On my HTSFF Twitter feed, for example, I post my latest free deals and retweet hot coupon codes and great links that other shoppers tell me about. Additionally, large retailers and manufacturers are using Twitter to interact with their consumers and alert them of discounts. That's very smart marketing, if you ask me. Retailers like Safeway and Whole Foods, along with manufacturers like Betty Crocker and ConAgra Foods, realized that connecting with consumers in real time would keep their products top of mind and that pushing hot coupons for new products would potentially boost sales. When you follow your favorite products or brands on Twitter, you often get rewarded with coupons and freebies.

Because Twitter can often be a traffic nightmare, coupon sites like Coupon Tweet and Cheap Tweet have popped up to help shoppers search the endless stream of Twitter deals by posting all the best coupon tweets in one central location. Both sites search Twitter for the latest, greatest real-time deals and then organize them all together on one user-friendly interface.

Facebook

Like they have done with Twitter, many retailers are using Facebook to build brand loyalty and launch new products. I'm a fan of this strategy because when you become a fan of many of these products, guess what—they send you coupons for free stuff.

Check out the sampling of random items I got for free just for giving them a little face time: a free deluxe fragrance sampler from Victoria's Secret, natural cat food from The Honest Kitchen, a chocolate almond latte from Einstein Bros Bagels, and even a free Jack Daniels Burger from Fridays. I'm telling you, the free deals are endless.

As we come to the end of the first chapter, I don't blame you if your head is spinning. That was a lot of information for the newly *How to Shop for Free* initiated. Take a deep breath and let it sink in. If there's only one take-away from what you've just read, I want it to be this: The tools for ridiculous savings are everywhere. Now, more than ever before, it's easier and more convenient to use coupons to get more of what you want for less.

To begin understanding what shopping for free is all about, complete the following simple assignment before moving on to the next chapter.

WORK IT: BUILD A STASH

Spend a few days getting your hands on as many inserts, loose coupons, and online printables as you can. Scan the local daily papers and the regional Sunday newspaper and pull out all the coupons. Look for individual coupons online and at your favorite stores. Pick them up at convenience stores and gas stations (look for peelies and tear pads on the refrigerator doors). Wherever you go—look around—you're probably not used to noticing them. Make a point of becoming aware of the promotional materials around you and start your own savings stash. Your husband and others close to you are going to think you've gone off the deep end, and that's a good sign. It means you're on your way to saving some serious cash.   ✄

Resources

8Coupons: www.8coupons.com (Mobile and printable coupons. This site promotes "the best deals on places to eat, drink, shop, and do stuff in your neighborhood." Users designate their zip codes and are shown deals in their areas and hot deals nationally. Selected coupons are loaded directly onto their cell phones.)

Cellfire: www.cellfire.com/ (Grocery, recipe, and Internet coupons for your savings card and your mobile phone. Coupons for Safeway, Kroger, King Soopers, Smith's, Frys, Vons, Ralph's, Dominicks)

Cheap Tweet: www.cheaptweet.com/ (Twitter deals, coupons, bargains, sales, and discounts. Cheap Tweet works similarly to Coupon Tweet by searching Twitter for the latest real-time deals and then organizing them all together on one user-friendly interface. The only real difference between the two is that Cheap Tweet encourages its users to vote on the deals, giving shoppers the opportunity to search for the deals that your peers have ranked the best.)

Coupon Sherpa: www.couponsherpa.com/ (This mobile application for the iPhone collects coupons from a variety of high-end retailers in your area and lets you access them in one place.)

Coupon Tweet: www.coupontweet.com/ (Find coupon codes, online coupons, and promotional codes from thousands of online stores on Twitter. This free site scours Twitter daily for coupon tweets in the categories of apparel, computers, tickets, travel, and groceries. The site locates thousands daily but posts only a percentage of the best (by their definition) deals on its site. Coupontweet.com's aim is to help you find up-to-the-minute coupons and discounts so you don't have to do any of the work. Sweet!)

Coupons.com: www.print.coupons.com (Grocery, recipe, and Internet coupons.)

Groupon: www.groupon.com/ (Offers one exclusive daily deal in your city from restaurants to car washes and small aircraft flying lessons. Once enough people sign up for the daily "get," the deal is on. Purchase the deal online and print your Groupon coupon.)

LivingSocial: http://livingsocial.com (Works very similarly to groupon. City-specific and featuring one deal a day with discounts of up to 90 percent at local restaurants, bars, spas, and theaters.)

P&GeSaver: www.pgesaver.com/ (P&G coupons and samples from P&GeSAVER and P&GbrandSAMPLER. Paper coupons are available in the monthly P&GbrandSAVER inserts.)

RedPlum: www.redplum.com/ (Coupons, contests, discounts, and deals. Paper coupons are available in the weekly RedPlum inserts or online.)

Shoptext: http://shoptext.com/ (Mobile coupons, free samples, and sweepstakes that you can enter via text message. Free to join.)

Shortcuts: http://shortcuts.com/ (Grocery and other coupons that load directly onto your savings cards.)

SmartSource: www.coupons.smartsource.com/ (Free coupons and discounts for top brands. Paper coupons are available in the weekly SmartSource inserts or online.)

Yowza: www.getyowza.com/ (Mobile coupons for the iPhone and iPod Touch, BlackBerry, Palm Pre, and Android. Yowza finds deals in your geographical area based on your consumer preferences. You select which stores and merchants you want Yowza to follow for you, and then you're alerted when great deals pop up. This iPhone app loads barcodes directly onto your iPhone that cashiers can scan at check out.)

2

Get It Together and Make a Plan

Shopping for free is a process, and I'm sure you understand that. But just in case you've already begun to plan your ten-day cruise to Cozumel with all the money you expect to save right away, I feel obligated to tell you that, in the beginning stages of this shopping game, you will continue to spend money on many of the things you need and would normally buy. That's right. Shopping for free doesn't happen overnight (morning-after hair and a bad hangover, maybe, but not a refrigerator stocked with free food and beverage). You'll need to make a plan. Consider it an investment in a future paved with free!

What's in the cart?

Here's what you'll find in this chapter:
- Tips for getting your budget in check
- Your personal number to beat
- How to stay organized
- The pre-shopping checklist
- The multiple store strategy

Review Your Budget

Before you can shop for free, it's imperative you take a very real look at how you've been budgeting your dollars up until now and set some realistic goals for the months ahead. When you set a personal goal that's achievable, it's less likely you'll become discouraged and give up. I'd hate for you to miss out on all the fun and financial freedom that goes along with shopping for free, so that's why we're going to take it one step at a time. Think of it this way: As you work your way up the *How to Shop for Free* ladder, you'll watch your expenses go down. And they absolutely will.

Before you can start budgeting for your favorite luxury items, you've got to master the basics. Let's examine what you spend in a month on groceries, household items, and toiletries. Not sure? Welcome to the check-out line. Most people don't keep track of what they spend in a month. If you *do* know, give yourself a gold star and move to the front of the line. For the rest of you who don't know where your money is going, it's time to do a reality check.

WORK IT: REALITY CHECK—REVIEW YOUR BUDGET

Okay ladies, gather your receipts, bank and credit card statements from the last month, along with a notebook and calculator. Apply booty to chair and no matter how cringe-inducing it is, toughen up, take a deep breath, and figure out to the penny how much you spent last month in the pharmacy and grocery stores. Tally it all up and write this number down. Be honest. Did you gasp? Want to get sick? Or shrug and say, "I knew it." Either way, know it's about to get better. Your grocery bill is only going to go down from here.   ✂

Amy, a 39 year-old *How to Shop for Free* beginner from Austin, Texas, needed help reviewing her budget. When I asked her how much she thought she spent on food, she was fairly confident she spent about

$400 a month on groceries for her family of three. After adding up all her expenses, she was shocked (and I think, a little horrified) to realize her monthly grocery costs totaled $989! It happens, shoppers. If you aren't paying attention, it's easy to overspend.

Once you've identified how much you spent last month, take a closer look at your receipts and identify *what* you bought. This is often when many shoppers are overcome with acute buyer's remorse. *Did I really need to try chocolate Cheerios?* If this is you, take it easy. Try not to beat yourself up too much. Chances are, you made several, if not many, spur of the moment purchases you could have lived without. Or paid top retail prices for items you suddenly ran out of and needed, like dishwashing detergent, diapers, or dental floss. Forgive yourself for past choices and make a pact with yourself that from this day forward—no more desperate shopping. With a little strategy and pre-planning you won't run out of essentials like toothpaste again. Or grab the latest fad food item.

Set a Goal

For the next few weeks, set a realistic goal to spend 20 percent less than you did last month. That's it—20 percent. If you were spending an average of $200 a week, then your new number to meet—or beat— is $160. Spending $160 isn't shopping for free, but it's a $40 difference. That's awesome. A difference in dollars means you're starting to get more and pay less.

Once you've mastered saving 20 percent, aim lower. If you saved 20 percent in January, challenge yourself to save 30 percent in February, 40 percent in March, and so on. You'll eventually reach a monthly spending budget that both satisfies and works for you. My personal grocery goal is four bucks a week; sixteen dollars a month. That said, I'm extremely disciplined and it took me a while to achieve this number. Allow yourself time to build up to your final

HOT TIP: Beat Your Own Number

When I first started shopping for free, I charged every shopping trip to my debit card so I could track each dollar I'd spent. Month to month, I'd challenge myself to beat that number. In no time at all, I'd cut my monthly bills in half. By having evidence of when and where you throw away money, you'll be more determined to reign in your spending like I did.　✂

goal. Hold that number in your mind and stay committed to it and I promise, you'll get there.

Get Organized

Now that you have your personal number to beat, I bet you're anxious to beat it. Not yet. Organization comes before shopping.

Pull out that stash of loose coupons, inserts, and promotional materials I asked you to start gathering. Spread everything out on your desk, dining room table, or kitchen counter. Let me take a guess—you're looking at a big mess of paper, aren't you? Don't panic; let's work to make sense of all your coupons.

Organization is key. As you've probably already discovered, once you start looking for savings, opportunities are everywhere, and if you don't have an organizational system in place, your stash of coupons, awards dollars, and sale advertisements will take over every available surface in your house. And that'll make most anyone go a little crazy.

How you organize your savings stash is ultimately up to you. I want you to develop a system that makes sense and fits into your lifestyle. Until you figure out what your personal style is, start by trying any one of these methods.

Envelopes

Create an envelope for each store you shop in. I regularly have marked envelopes for Shaw's, Walmart, CVS, Market Basket, and Stop & Shop stuffed into my Coach purse. My envelopes are packed with the latest savings opportunities at each store and when I want to shop, they're good to go.

Pros: This is a simple system and doesn't cost you much to implement (in fact, envelopes are often on sale, and with a coupon, free). You can also use zip-top storage bags in much the same way.

Cons: The downside to using envelopes or baggies is that they rip and can start to look a little trashed.

SHOPPER'S

Hall of Fame

"My husband and I have turned saving money into a contest. We keep track each month of how much we've saved (and which one of us "found" the most savings) and the loser has to do something for the other the next month. In our house, more often than not, that means doing the dishes. Plus, the savings at the end of the month is usually enough to get us an extra date night. Bonus!"

Blythe, Comanche, Oklahoma

"I have been staying home for four years now and shopping for free for three. With our household income cut in half, we have been able to put money into savings and to enjoy simple luxuries like weekly meals out. I attribute this in large part to the money I have saved by shopping this way. I can't imagine ever going back to paying full price for things now that I know I don't have to. Why waste our money?"

Lori, Dover, New Hampshire

Accordion File

A step-up from the basic envelope is an accordion file. You can easily file your coupons in an accordion file by expiration date, by store, and/or by products. The accordion file is neat and tidy, and many of them will fit right into your purse. When you "google" accordion file, you'll discover that many companies have given this style a modern look. Vibrant colors, cool patterns, and various shapes and sizes have transformed an old office staple into a cool accessory.

Pros: I used an accordion file before I stepped up my shopping game to extreme shopper. I dedicated the front slot to the particular store I was shopping in; my coupons were right there and ready, and I didn't have to dig around in the check-out line.

Cons: The downside to using an accordion file is that you can only jam so much into one and if you drop it, expect everything to come flying out and flutter to the floor while you crawl after your coupons cursing. Zippered pockets on an accordion file would be a great invention; you heard it here first.

Binder

Many *How to Shop for Free* shoppers use the binder method. It involves clipping, or printing, your coupons and slipping them into plastic pages (baseball card trading sheets, currency holders, and blank photo albums work well) that you organize into one binder.

Pros: The upside to the binder is that you have all your savings meticulously organized in one place.

Cons: The downside is that it's big and bulky, and, to be honest, a grown woman carting around a Trapper Keeper isn't a great look. Functional: yes. Sophisticated and sexy: no.

Savings Box

Your local container store, is a great place to find a customized coupon box. I recommend going with a size that will fit into the top basket of your grocery cart—you know, where you put your purse and the produce you don't want to get smashed. That way, you can have it right in front of you when you shop. Many shoppers create dividers to separate their coupons within the box by store and/or products.

Pros: The box gives you easy access to your savings.

Cons: Like the binder, it's clunky (I've seen coupon boxes the size of something my husband keeps all his tools in) and just one more thing you have to cart around with you in the grocery store. If you're already carrying a purse, a gym bag, a laptop, or a baby, the savings box might just be that one extra accessory that puts you over the edge.

Filing

This is my favorite way to go about it. Remember: I'm not big on clipping. Well, at least not until I'm ready to shop like I mean it. When I first started using the filing method, I put my unclipped Sunday inserts in stackable letter trays, but my stockpile quickly outgrew the trays. I've since upgraded to a large, filing cabinet. On any given Sunday, I take my stack of RedPlum (RP), SmartSource (SS), Procter & Gamble (PG), and General Mills (GM) inserts and file them into dedicated folders that include the date they were distributed. My folders for a Sunday in March might be labeled like this: 3/14 RP, 3/14 SS, 3/14 PG, and so on. I file these folders away in my cabinet. Each cabinet drawer (there are three) is dedicated to a specific month—April, May, June, for example.

You might be thinking, *Holy Moly. That's A LOT of coupons. How does she remember what she's got in that filing cabinet?* It's true that I have a crazy number of coupons and way more than I could ever keep filed away in my *own* memory folder. This is why I rely on my super duper coupon database on www.howtoshopforfree.net to keep it all straight.

Pros: Filing inserts away by date until you're ready to clip is the most streamlined method I've found to keep my coupons organized.

Cons: You must have access to a coupon database to make this method work. The good news is that the coupon database on www.howtoshop forfree.net is super easy to understand and free to everyone.

The *How to Shop for Free* Coupon Database

When I notice there's a sale on a product I use, I go to the coupon database I've set up on www.howtoshopforfree.net and type in the name of the product in the search field to see if a coupon for that product exists. (Again, the coupon database is free and available to anyone who wants to use it.) For example, I notice that PetSmart is having a sale on Iams dog food, and, because I have a dog that eats like a horse, getting a good deal on kibble catches my attention right away. I type "Iams" into the www.howtoshopforfree.net database and if a coupon for Iams dog food exists—presto—it'll pop up. I can also search by date and/or coupon value. All in all, the database will tell me the value of savings, the expiration date, when it was published, and what the source of the coupon is. It might look like this:

Iams Dry Dog Food $1.00   5/31/10   PG 3/14/10

This Procter & Gamble coupon has a $1.00 value and will expire on May 31. Having a coupon database to turn to is why my filing system works wonders for me. After the database tells me when my coupon came out, for example, 3/14 PG, I open up my filing cabinet and pull out all the PG inserts from the week of March 14th. I go through each insert until I find the coupon I'm looking for—in this case Iams dog food—and I pull the coupon out of each insert. Once

I've collected them all, I stack them together and start cutting. Depending on how many inserts I've gotten my hands on for that particular week, (I might have five, ten, or twenty) all my Iams dog food coupons drop out together. I stick them in an envelope dedicated to Pet Smart, and now I'm ready to shop.

I think I'd go out of my mind if I couldn't refer to the coupon database on www.howtoshopforfree.net. Thanks to the Internet and some of my more frugalista members who have done all the work for you by keeping the *How to Shop for Free* database updated with all the latest and greatest deals, all you have to do is know what you're looking for and type it in.

You Asked It

Q: *How long does this take? Prepping to shop seems like it requires a considerable amount of time.*

A: *Shopping for free does take time and I totally get it if you find yourself getting antsy during this first stage of the game, but I hope you'll be patient. Shopping for free takes this sort of up-front planning (which equals time), but it does pay off. Not buying it yet? Maybe this'll change your mind: Since getting Harry, our yellow Labrador nearly four years ago, I've only bought dog food once—and he eats the good stuff. I'll never forget the day I used a stack of coupons at Pet Smart to score forty bags of dog food for nothing (shoppers, that's a $500 value). My cart was so heavy I could barely push it out the door and to the car. My husband used to complain, "Having pets is too expensive." Not with these kind of deals, honey!*

Getting an organizational system in place might sound like a time-suck, but it'll ultimately save you many hours. I spend about five hours every week cruising circulars, surfing online deals, checking the database, and printing and cutting coupons. That might seem like a lot of time to you, and, admittedly, I'm more obsessed and addicted to shopping for free than most, but while five hours of prep time might be time you don't *think* you have, realize this: The time you spend pre-shopping will save you time in the store. With a list and a spending plan in place, you're not going to be poking around in the aisles, tempted to reach for stuff you don't need. Those days are over. You shop with purpose and conviction now. When you enter a store, you do so with one goal in mind: Get the best deals and get out.

SHOPPER'S
Hall of Fame

"I would have to say the biggest change that I had to make for this to work for me was understanding how important it is to change your mindset on how to shop. Patience! Too many want to make this work for them immediately. They don't understand that it is gradual at first. I'm barely four months into shopping for free, and it is just now hitting home what I've accomplished so far. It is quite noticeable in my cupboards, bank account, and the modest stockpile that I have acquired. I used to spend $500 on monthly groceries. Now I spend $130."

Jen, Ann Arbor, Michigan

"The great thing about these techniques is that they work for both the beginner and more advanced saver. Kathy has changed the way I think about everyday shopping, as well as planning in advance for future items. Her methods are more than just how to save a few bucks here and there . . . it's a lifestyle change. My household has saved hundreds just by using some of the more simple techniques."

Pete, Atkinson, New Hampshire

Ready, Set, Get Shopping

I'm nearly ready to unleash you into the aisles, but not before you make a list and check it twice.

Make a List

Make a list of all the items you plan on purchasing on your next shopping trip: groceries and dry goods. Include your most popular staples, too. In my house, this is peanut butter and ketchup. My kids can't get enough of either and often confuse the two. My ten-year-old is known for putting peanut butter on his corn on the cob and ketchup on his toast.

Check Store Ads

Next, scan your weekly store ads, either online or in the newspaper. You've been collecting all these, right? Do you see anything on sale that's also on your list? Make a checkmark next to those items. Wait a minute—did you just say that there's nothing on sale that you would ever use? Let's pause for a minute here so I can say a few words about brand loyalty. There are going to be some products (I'm guessing makeup and hair products for most women) that many of you are loyal to, and no one's going to talk you into trying something else, even if it's half the price or free. Fine. I'm not going to pressure you to stop using your favorite age-defying night cream. I will say, however, that there are probably many things you're in the *habit* of using, but not necessarily committed to.

Let me give you an example. I've always loved LAY's sour cream and onion flavored potato chips. When I'm having a nasty craving for salt, I reach for the LAY's. Correction: I lunge for the LAY's. Well, not too long ago, I started seeing coupons for Quaker mini rice cakes in sour cream and onion flavor. Around the same time these coupons were popping up everywhere, Quaker mini rice cakes went on sale at my local market. I realized that if I were to combine the coupon with the sale, they'd be free. I don't ever pass on free, so I picked up three bags. Well, let me tell you, those little cardboard snacks are delicious—and healthy. I like them better than my LAY's! If I'd stayed true to my brand, I wouldn't have discovered something new that I now love or gotten such a great deal.

You will find that shopping for free is easier when you suspend your brand loyalty from time to time. And you might find that you *become* brand loyal to a product, like I have with my mini rice cakes, because of coupons. Because coupons are issued by all kinds of companies making gobs of different products, the more you're willing to experiment, the more you'll save. Plus, if something works out to be free, or nearly free, what's the harm in giving it a try?

Match Sales with Savings

Go back through your store ads one more time. Are there any products on sale that you'd be willing to try if you could get them for free, or nearly free? Add them to your shopping list. Now, break out that stash of coupons you've been collecting and/or search for coupons in the www.howtoshopforfree.net database that match what's on your list. Any lucky combinations? Bingo! Once you start matching coupons with sales, you'll be shopping for free in no time. Be warned: Combining coupons with promotions and sales can be confusing at first, so don't throw a fit if you're not getting it. A three-year-old having a meltdown in the ice cream section is one thing. A grown woman having one in the check-out line is quite another. I'll give you the complete lowdown on mixing, matching, stacking, and doubling coupons in Chapter 3: Woo Hoo Deal Alert. For now, pick yourself up off the virtual floor of aisle ten and let's move on.

Check Your List Twice

Rewrite your original shopping list and scratch off any items that aren't on sale or that you don't have coupons for. *Okay*, you don't have to take them all off. If you need tampons, you *need* tampons. Try removing one or two items this first go-round. I get that not everything you need, or want to buy, is going to have a corresponding coupon or be on sale. Like I said: In the beginning stages of this shopping game, you will continue to spend money on many of the things you need and would normally buy. That said, every time you pick up an item, you have a decision to make. Do I really *need* it now? Or do I just *want* it now? If you don't need it, then do yourself a favor and put it back on the shelf. Why pay top dollar for something you don't need today that'll go on sale tomorrow? I don't care what it is—green tea, string cheese, or zinc lozenges—eventually every item on your shopping list will go on sale, and that's when you buy it. Got it? If you stick to your list and your number to beat, you will save money every time you shop.

HOT TIP: Do Your Math

Do your math ahead of time or you're likely to blow it. I say this from experience, which is why I've gotten into the habit of figuring out my total cost of what I plan to buy before I head to the store. By doing the math ahead of time, I'm more likely to stay on budget and resist impulse buys. Also, if you know your total ahead of time, if items aren't scanned properly at the register, or if the correct amounts aren't deducted from your total after coupons, you'll know it. If my total comes to seventeen dollars and I've estimated for four, I know something isn't right, and I'll make sure it's corrected. Most shoppers just slide through their debit card, totally unaware if they've been overcharged because they're not paying attention and they haven't done their prep work. From here on, you're in charge—not being charged. ✂

Checklist:
Ready, Set, Get Shopping

- ✓ Make a Shopping List. Include items you need today along with your favorite staples.
- ✓ Check Weekly Store Ads. Are there any items on sale that you buy on a regular basis? Make a checkmark next to those items.
- ✓ Match Savings with Sales. Do you have any coupons that correspond to a sale item? When you match coupons with sales, you maximize your savings in a big way.
- ✓ Check Your List Twice. Rewrite your original shopping list and scratch off any items that aren't on sale, that you don't have coupons for, or that you don't actually need today.

WORK IT: ONLY PAY IN CASH

You're not quite seasoned enough, but after you've tracked your purchases for a month or two and learned how to meet and beat your own number, try "upping" your shopping game by paying for your purchases only in cash. For example, if you "guesstimate" that after coupons and additional savings, your out-of-pocket (OOP) costs will be fifty-seven bucks, only take sixty dollars in cash with you to the store. This might seem a little reckless and scary. Having just enough money on hand is a gamble and no one wants to run out of money in the check-out line, but I'm willing to bet that if you use this strategy, you'll stop throwing empty calorie snack foods or other unnecessary random items into your basket.   ✁

Pull on Your Big Girl Pants

Now that you have your list, a plan, and coupons in hand, I want you to pull on your big girl pants and shop with your head held up high.

If you're new to this, my guess is you might be feeling a little gun-shy or embarrassed about handing a cashier a big wad of coupons. It's totally normal if you are. Since many of us are conditioned to avoid coupons like the H1N1 virus, I recommend recruiting a shopping buddy right away, a girlfriend who also wants to learn how to shop for free. In the beginning, shop in pairs, scope out similar deals, and set matching goals. This will help you stay motivated, brave, and when your weekly bills start to shrink before your very eyes, you'll have someone to high-five in the check-out line—and splurge with on that mani/pedi.

Pick Your Stores

The old you might be the kind of woman who gets everything she needs at one store because she thinks she doesn't have time to shop in multiple stores.

Stop right there. I want you to take *time* out of it. I shop at multiple stores because I can get more free stuff that way. Period. Every week, different stores have different deals that work out for free. The way I see it, I can't afford to miss out on any of them. Plus, now that you're aware that the time you spend prepping to shop cuts down on actual shopping time, hitting multiple stores shouldn't discourage you.

Weekly, I shop at CVS, Stop & Shop, Shaw's, and Market Basket (the last two are East Coast supermarket chains). Sure, I may spend a little extra gas driving from place to place, but what I spend in gas, I more than make up in overall savings (plus, I've figured out a way to get gas for free and I'll tell you about that in Chapter 5: Like Getting Paid to Shop.) Some weeks, I spread my shopping out over several days. Other times, I do it all in one day. Only you know how much available time you have, or are willing to make, and I trust that you'll figure out a schedule and rhythm that works for you. But know this: With a list and a plan in place, you'll be surprised how much faster your shopping trips will be. I shop faster than anyone I know, and soon you'll be saying that, too. You might also be surprised by the extra calories you burn. Shopping for free builds a sweat not unlike the afterglow from a spinning class—minus the tight-fitting biker shorts. Even when I'm hitting three to four stores, I can knock it out in a few hours because I stick to my list and my personal number to beat.

Before we move on to Chapter 3: Woo Hoo Deal Alert, I want to share a personal story. I think it'll shed some light on why I spend (or don't spend) the way I do.

Several years ago, my husband Brian, who works for a nearby city, was up for a promotion when he was hit with a winter flu that, within days, took a nasty turn toward acute bronchitis and escalated into life-threatening pneumonia. He is the primary breadwinner for our family of six, and his medical bills and three-month absence from work hit us very hard financially.

During Brian's recovery, I started scheming ways we could spend less and save more. We'd just had a baby, and I really wanted to stay home with this one. I knew that if Brian got passed up for the promotion, there'd be no chance of that.

I'd always followed store sales and casually clipped coupons, but saving money wasn't a "lifestyle choice," per se, until one afternoon, when my mindset shifted. I had run into a convenience store to pick up some juice. I found a carton of Old Orchard cranberry that was on sale for a dollar, and I just happened to have three coupons for the same thing in my wallet. The coupons gave me a dollar off one bottle of juice, so guess what—I picked up three bottles for free. That's when the light went on upstairs. I thought, "What if I applied this strategy to more than just cranberry juice? What more could I get for nothing?" From that day forward, I began challenging myself to shop for free. I soon learned how to get food, cleaning supplies, and cosmetics for free. Then I tackled baby products, pet food, school supplies, and housewares. I then took it up a notch and mastered shopping for clothes, electronics, and prescriptions for next to nothing.

Today, we look like we have it all, and a lot of it is a lifestyle built on coupons. We live in a 2,800-square-foot Colonial-style home on nearly three acres of land. My husband and I drive vehicles that we paid for in cash. My kids and I wear high-end labels. Our oldest is in college, and we have no credit card debt. What's more, my husband and I never fight about money. *How many married couples can say that?* The irony is that my husband never got his promotion; he still works for the city making $45,000 a year. And yet, to take a walk through our house and sit down at our dinner table, you'd never know that "on paper," we're considered low-income. We live a life of abundance because I've discovered the secret to shopping for free.

Whatever your reason for reading this book—maybe you're working to get out of debt, maintain or improve your current lifestyle, or simply survive day-to-day—understand this: *More* money isn't the answer. *Saving* money is. Getting more for less is a matter of changing how you think.

3

Woo Hoo Deal Alert

How'd you do? Did you get some great deals? Or did you walk away thinking, "I don't think I did that right. I was supposed to get a protein bar for free and I ended up *buying* three!" If I'm describing something similar to your first "shopping-for-free" experience, try not to be discouraged and realize that shopping for free is a numbers game. It's probably going to take you a few tries before you totally get it. Give yourself permission to bang your head against the wall the first few times. I'm pushing you to think about shopping in a new way, one that takes some pre-planning and a little arithmetic.

Throughout the pages that follow, I'll continue to push you further by showing you the many ways you can get something for nothing and how to improve your game. This is an important chapter, so I encourage you to take your time with it. You might even want to jot down a few notes as you go along. Be sure you understand each savings strategy before you move on to the next.

What's in the cart?

Here's what you'll find in this chapter:
- The difference between combining and doubling coupons
- Advanced mix and match strategies
- The secret to buy one get one deals
- How to make rain checks and rebates work for you
- Cashier etiquette
- More coupon lingo!

Combining Coupons

There's a popular shopping myth that says coupons cannot be combined. Not true, shoppers. This is how I get so much loot for mere pennies. Combining coupons, or stacking, can be an exhilarating high, and once you get the hang of it, you're likely to feel as if you're on a winning streak at the Black Jack table. The savings really add up when a weekly special matches a product that you already have a coupon, or coupons, for. In many cases, matching manufacturer coupons with store sales = FREE. That said, there is a right and a wrong way to do this, so pay attention. It's not a complete free-for-all.

Here's how it works: You can combine store and manufacturer coupons (MFR Qs) to get items for a fraction of their original retail price. For example, say Target is selling 12-packs of Pure Life bottled water for $4.00. If you have a Target store coupon for $1.00 off Pure Life and an MFR coupon for $3.00 off, you could use them together to get the water at Target for free. Here's the breakdown:

12-pack of bottled water	$4.00
Target store coupon	− $1.00 off
MFR coupon	− $3.00 off
	= FREE

HOT TIP: Don't Let the Pictures Fool You

If a coupon says *Save $2.00 on Any Oscar Mayer Cold Cut* and the coupon shows you a picture of traditional pink bologna, that doesn't mean you have to buy bologna to get the deal. If it says any, it means ANY: turkey breast, salami, Virginia ham, whatever. Ignore the pictures and read the words. Oscar Mayer, like many brands, makes a lot of products. They can't all fit in the picture. ✂

Here's another one:

L'Oréal lipstick sale price	$3.99
Walgreens store coupon	– $2.00 off
L'Oréal MFR coupon	– $2.00 off
	= FREE

Are you starting to see how to mix and match a winning combination? I told you your rudimentary math skills would come in handy.

You Asked It

Q: *I have a Babies R Us store coupon for $10 off when you buy two packs of any Huggies diapers. I also have two manufacturer coupons for $3.00 off a single pack. Can I use all three coupons?*

A: *Yes. This combination is a little more sophisticated, but it's still a green light at checkout. You can use two manufacturer coupons because you are buying two items. In this case, you apply one MFR coupon to each. In the following shopping scenario, you can combine the store and manufacturer*

SHOPPER'S HALL OF SHAME

Combining Like Coupons

You cannot use two manufacturer coupons together on a single item. For example, it's a no-no to combine two L'Oréal MFR coupons on one L'Oréal lipstick. Likewise, you cannot apply two store coupons to a single item. You can ONLY combine a single MFR coupon + single store coupon on a single item. These are independent discounts that you can use together for a bigger savings. One discount is from the manufacturer and the other from the store.

Once again:

L'Oréal lipstick sale price	$3.99
Two L'Oréal MFR Qs @	− $2.00 off
	= NO CAN DO

---

coupons and get two packs of Huggies for $16.00 off your total bill. Not free, but we're working up to that. Here's what it looks like:

Huggies $10.99 x 2 packs	= $21.98
Babies R Us discount on 2 packs	− $10.00
MFR discount on 2 packs	− $6.00
TOTAL	= $5.98 for 2 packs

You buy two packs and get the store discount of $10.00 off. You then apply the MFR coupons of $3.00 off/1 to each of those packs. Get it?

WORK IT: GO FISH!

Compare this week's store sales and store coupons to the manufacturer coupons in your Sunday inserts and/or the coupon database at www.howtoshopforfree.net and see what works out for free, or nearly free. All you need this next go-round is one winning combination.

Remember the card game Go Fish? If Amy's Naturals Vegetable Soup is on sale at your local market for $0.99, and you have an MFR Q for $1.00 off, then guess what—free soup!   ✂

Buying in Multiples

Buying in multiples simply means using multiple coupons (also called "stacking") to get more than one of the same item. Despite what you've been led to believe, this, too, is perfectly legit.

Multiple Coupons

For example, let's say you have ten coupons for $0.50 off/1 box of Kashi TLC bars. It would be perfectly acceptable to throw ten boxes of Kashi TLC bars into your cart and apply all ten coupons toward your order at checkout, one coupon per box.

SHOPPER'S
Hall of *Fame*

"Shopping for free really works. I've been doing it for over four years now. It may take a bit of hard work and determination at first, but eventually you will be a pro and be able to quickly scan the store circulars each week and know what will work out free or close to free. The time you spend learning now will really pay off in the end. Before you know it, your pantry and storage areas will be stocked with the things you use everyday. The savings are endless. Plus, shopping for free can be a lot of fun. Before I started this I used to hate shopping and put off going to the store as much as possible. Now I enjoy the thrill of the hunt for bargains to see how much money I can save for my family."

Michelle, Waterloo, Illinois

Here's how it works:

10 boxes of Kashi TLC x $2.59/box	= $25.90
10 MFR coupons @ $0.50 off: 10 x $0.50	− $5.00
TOTAL	= $20.90

Or if you're feeling really bold, you could use TWO coupons per box if one is a manufacturer coupon and one is an in-store coupon. Theoretically, you could use twenty coupons on ten boxes of bars for a total savings of fifteen bucks. Girls, this is why having multiple coupons is a smart shopping strategy.

Here's the second shopping scenario:

10 boxes of Kashi TLC Bars: 10 x $2.59/box	= $25.90
10 MFR coupons @ $0.50 off: 10 x .50	− $5.00
10 store coupons @ $1.00 off: 10 x $1.00	− $10.00
TOTAL = $10.90 (just a little over a buck a box)	

This type of equation tends to confuse newbie shoppers, and I can almost feel you scratching your head over this, too. If a coupon says one *per purchase*, doesn't that mean you can't use more than one? Good catch and I agree with you that the language is sometimes tricky. Many shoppers confuse "per purchase" with "per transaction." Per purchase means that only one of the same coupon ($0.50 off/1 box of Kashi bars) can be applied to each single purchase (one box of Kashi bars).

Per transaction means you can only use one coupon ($0.50 off/ 1 box of Kashi bars) per store visit. There is a way around this restrictive rule, and my friend Larry showed me how. He had a stack of $1.00-off MFR coupons he wanted to use toward a sale on Right Guard Deodorant. When he was told that he could only use one of his "per transaction" coupons per visit, he said, "Let me get this right. You're saying that I can only use one coupon now, but the next time

HOT TIP: Separate Your Orders

Said a different way, per transaction means per register receipt, so if you don't want to walk in and out of stores all day long like Larry, you can get around this rule another way. For example, if you're buying five Right Guard deodorants and using five "per-transaction" coupons, you can simply separate your order using those plastic divider things at the check-out stand, creating a separate receipt for each of the five deodorants. A little obnoxious? Maybe for the person standing behind you, but it works, and you're not breaking any store rules doing it this way. ✂

I come into the store I can buy another Right Guard Deodorant and apply another coupon toward it then?" When they told him that was correct, he walked out the door, turned around, and walked right back in and said, "I'M BACK!!! Although the store didn't find the humor in Larry's mockery of the rules, they had to honor his next "transaction" because it was, technically, a return visit.

You Asked It

Because there are legal no-no's when shopping for free, nervous members sometimes have questions, like:

Q: *Before knowing the rules about multiples, I'd often hand cashiers two or three MFR coupons to apply to one item and most of the time, they would pass them right through. I assumed I could do this.*

A: *A lot of cashiers don't even bother looking at the coupons they scan, so you can't assume it's right just because they scan through. More importantly, if*

a cashier scans through two MFR coupons for the same item, the manu-
facturer might not reimburse the store and that's considered a loss. My
worry is that if stores start losing money due to coupon fraud, they'll restrict
coupon use, or heaven forbid, shut it down altogether. Talk about a day
of mourning!

If you know you are mixing, matching, and combining coupons in
the wrong way: STOP. The last time I checked, the penalties for those
shoppers convicted of coupon fraud didn't look like a walk through your
favorite boutique. Prison sentences of three to five years are not uncommon.
Financial penalties generally vary but have often been in excess of
$200,000, and there's no coupon for that.

Multiple Orders: When You Buy (WYB)

Another type of multiple-order scenario is the When You Buy, or
WYB, deal. Basically, it means Get X when you buy Y.

Give it a try:

If the deal is, *Get $1.00 off when you buy 3 boxes of Cheerios*, can
you use three $1.00 off coupons, getting $1.00 off of each box?

If you answered No, you're correct. You're learning fast. If the
coupon says $1.00 off 3, you need to purchase three boxes to get
the deal.

SHOPPER'S HALL OF SHAME
Using Multiples

You cannot use more than one of the *same* coupon per item.
So, if you have three coupons for a $0.75 off/1 box of Kleenex,
you can't use all three coupons on one box. Make sense? Not
only is this against the rules, but it's illegal. It's coupon fraud.
(For the complete low-down on coupon fraud, skip to Chapter 7: Scams, Cheats, and Big Time Couponing No-No's.)

Try it again:

You have several MFR coupons for $0.50 off/2 Snickers Bars. They're on sale for $0.50 a piece. Can you use two coupons and get both Snickers for free?

No! The coupon states that you must buy two in order to get the discount of 50 cents. If you wanted to use two coupons, you would have to buy four Snickers and it would look like this:

Snickers Bar @$0.50 x 4	= $2.00
Two MFR coupons @$0.50 off/2	– $1.00
TOTAL	= $1.00 for four Snickers

Still one heck of a deal, but not *free*. If your store doubled coupons up to $0.99, however, they would all be free. That's the kind of deal I jump on.

Double Up

Even though you can't use two of the same coupon on a single item, the "value" of a coupon can often be doubled and applied to a single item. This is called "doubling" coupons. Not all stores do this, but many will. Some even triple coupons and these are the stores I love almost more than my own children. How it works:

Let's say, I throw a frozen gourmet pizza that's on sale for $1.00 into my cart. I have a $0.50-off coupon that the store will double, making the pizza free. Are you thinking what I'm thinking? Pizza Party! With four more $0.50-off/1 coupons, I could bag five free pizzas without spending a dime.

Like I said, not all stores double coupons, so you must ask your cashier or look online and see what your store's policy is on doubling. You can't expect every cashier at every store to double a coupon. It's either the store policy to allow it or not, so do your homework.

SHOPPER'S HALL OF SHAME

Do Not Double Means Do Not Double

If a coupon says "DO NOT DOUBLE" on it, the store or the manufacturer doesn't want you to double it. End of story. Like "per transaction," these coupons take the fun out of the shopping game and the sometimes spoiled sport in me will simply toss them aside (and you know how I feel about throwing coupons away).

Save yourself the pink face that goes along with a cashier who looks at you sideways and hands you back your coupons.

What's the Value?

Find out the value of the coupon the store will double up to. For example, a local store I frequent will double coupons up to a $0.99 value. So, if I have a $0.50-off coupon, it'll double to $1.00 off. A $0.75-off coupon will double to $1.50 off. And a $0.99-off coupon doubles to $1.98 off (although $0.99 coupons are as rare as a grocery store without Muzak).

Here's how it works:

Trident gum regular $1.49
MFR coupon @$0.75, doubled to $1.50
TOTAL   = FREE

Wait. It gets even better. A popular superstore in my area (and I'm sure there's one close to where you live, too) has special double coupon days where they'll double up to $2.00. This is an uber-Woo Hoo Deal Alert! The last time I cashed in on this deal, I walked away with a cart full of shampoo, conditioner, hairspray, hair color, panty liners, tampons, toothbrushes, dental floss, razors, body soap, Ziploc bags, Saran Wrap, tin foil, Windex, laundry soap, fabric softener, Clorox wipes, 409, Carpet Fresh, toilet cleaner, sponges, dish soap, oatmeal, cereal, snack bars, candles, Glade Air Freshener, cat food, cat treats, cat litter, dog bones, beef jerky, tuna fish, baby wipes, baby oil, baby food, kids soap, flavored water, bug spray, and sun tan lotion for nothing. I had $2.00-off coupons that doubled to $4.00, making each item free. Search for stores that double high-value coupons and if you aren't already shopping there, I suggest you start.

You Asked It

Q: *If it's the store policy to double, does it automatically happen? Or do you have to quietly ask the cashier to double it?*

A: *If a coupon is "doubable" (yes, I made that word up), then it will automatically double. No secret handshake required.*

SHOPPER'S
Hall of Fame

"I became a stay-at-home mom four years ago when my son was born. Quitting my job cut our family's income in half. The sacrifice was worth it, but things were very tight for us. A friend of mine told me about How to Shop for Free, but I doubted her and told her that nothing is free. That was about three years ago. Since then, I have saved our family thousands of dollars. I have changed the way I shop. I buy what is on sale that I can combine with a coupon and get for free or nearly free. I have stockpiles of everything and can go without a trip to the store (other than for milk or produce) for at least a month."

Lori, Dover, New Hampshire

Once you've found out whether or not your store doubles coupons and the value they double up to, find out *how many* of the same coupon they'll double in a single visit. Six seems to be the magic number where I live. I can double up to six "like" coupons, meaning six of the same barcode up to $0.99 cents. Again, you can usually find this information online or in the store's flyer. Be sure you're getting the right info for your particular store. Policies can sometimes vary even in the same zip code. Again, it pays (really) to do your homework.

Doubling Up: What Would You Do?

Your store doubles coupons up to $0.50. You want to purchase a can of Muir Glen tomato paste priced at $1.00. You have a coupon for $1.00 off two cans and a coupon for $0.50 off of one. Which coupon do you use?

Use the $0.50 off of one can.

1 can of Muir Glen tomato paste	$1.00
MFR coupon @ $0.50 doubles to	− $1.00
TOTAL	= FREE

If you use the $1.00 off of two cans, you must purchase two cans to get the deal and it looks like this:

2 cans of Muir Glen tomato paste	$2.00
MFR coupon @ $1.00 off/2 cans	− $1.00
TOTAL	= $1.00 or $0.50 per can

You Asked It

Q: If a store is having a Buy 10 for $10.00 sale, do I have to buy all ten items to get the sale price?

A: No. And most people don't know this and often end up buying ten cans of black beans when they really only needed two. Unless the shelf tag *clearly states:* Must Buy (this many) to get (the sale price), *you can choose to buy as many or as few as you'd like. So, if black beans are on sale 10/$10 you can opt to buy 1 can for $1.00 . . . 2 for $2.00 . . . 3 for $3.00, etc.*

That said, a 10 for $10 sale is a good deal, especially if you have $0.50-off coupons that will double. Imagine this awesome bean fest:

Black Beans 10 for $10 sale
Buy five cans @ $1 each   = $5.00
Use five $0.50-off coupons that double   − $5.00
TOTAL   = FREE

Buy One Get One

The Buy One Get One deal, once mastered, will take your shopping experience to a whole new level of amazing. Buy One, Get One, or BOGO, means you must purchase one item to get a second item at a discounted price. You see this kind of deal with cereal all the time. For

---

SHOPPER'S
Hall of Fame

"At first shopping for free was confusing—learning all the new terminology, (OYNO, OOP, BOGO), matching coupons with sales, stacking, stockpiling, etc. But within just a couple of weeks, I created my own coupon file and armed with what I learned on www.howtoshopforfree.net, I made my first few purchases. The first couple of times, I was so nervous. I was sweating and shaking all over the place because I just felt this was too good to be true. But after a couple of transactions, I felt more confident, and I've since become quite a pro at it."

Regina, Gainsville, Florida

example, *Buy any one General Mills cereal; get the second box free.* You must buy one box at its regular retail price to get the second one free. Make sense?

You're already getting a deal on a BOGO, and if you can stack coupons on top of that, the deal gets even sweeter. Let's say you have a manufacturer coupon for $2 off General Mills cereal. You would buy one box at the original price and get the second one free. Adding in the coupon, you'd get two bucks off the box you're paying for. It would look like this:

General Mills Cheerios, Buy one@	$4.49
Get the second box free	$ .00
MFR coupon @	– $2.00 off
TOTAL:	$2.49 for two boxes

Basically, the store is giving you one for free, and the manufacturer is giving you the discount on the one you're purchasing. This is a good deal, but it's not free, so let's look at another shopping scenario:

Your local store has a *Buy One Stonyfield Yogurt, Get One Free* deal and you have an MFR coupon for *Buy two, get $1.00 off.*

Two Stonyfield yogurts @ $0.99 each	= $1.98
Store will credit you	– $0.99 (BOGO)
MFR coupon gives you	– $1.00 off
TOTAL	= FREE

Even though one is free, you're technically buying both. Keep in mind that anything scanned is considered to be a purchase. If it's a "purchase," you're allowed to apply a coupon toward it. To quell any worries that I'm encouraging shady behavior here, it is absolutely not coupon fraud for a store to accept a coupon on a "free" item. From a legal standpoint, you are still purchasing the item.

Try this combination:

Your local store has a Buy One ALL Detergent @ $3.99, Get One Free. You have two MFR coupons for $2.00 off/1 bottle. You use both coupons to get both for free. Here's how:

ALL Detergent $3.99 x 2	= $7.98
Store BOGO deal	– $3.99
MFR coupon	– $2.00 off 1
MFR coupon	– $2.00 off 1
TOTAL	= FREE

Most stores will allow you to use two MFR coupons on a BOGO deal because again, technically, you're "purchasing" two items, and you can use one MFR coupon toward every one item purchased. If you feel your head spinning over this, rest assured that BOGO deals are some of the hardest to get mentally, but once you do, the savings are significant. In other words—learning how to work a BOGO deal is worth your time.

WORK IT: BUY ONE GET ONE: BOGO

Search the www.howtoshopforfree.net coupon database for BOGO deals. Type in BOGO and leave all other fields blank. All current BOGO deals will pop up. Find a BOGO deal for a product you'd normally buy and use it on your next shopping trip to get two products for the price of one.

If BOGOs make you feel like a DODO, each time you're working one, ask yourself, *What is this coupon requiring me to buy to use it?* The more you work BOGO deals, the faster you'll get it. When in doubt, go to www.howtoshopforfree.net and ask the group. There's always a lively forum discussion going on about a current BOGO deal.   ✂

The craziest (in the best way) BOGO deal is if a store is having a BOGO sale and you have a BOGO manufacturer coupon for the same product. Jackpot! The store is giving you one item for free, and the manufacturer is giving you the second item for free. This is an absolutely legal transaction. The result: two products for nothing. Feels a little naughty doesn't it? Contrary to how it might feel, the stores are not losing any money when you walk out the door with free loot, so relax. Stores are reimbursed by the manufacturer for every coupon redeemed. Unfortunately, not all cashiers understand this. Some *will* think you're trying to pull a fast one. If this happens, politely ask them to refer to their store policy. I've debated this with a handful of store managers who, once they read their own BOGO policy, want to cash in on the deal, too.

According to many extreme shoppers, BOGO deals are *the* reason you want to collect multiple inserts or print more than one of the same BOGO coupon. If your favorite laundry detergent (which is never cheap, or so you thought) is on sale, Buy One, Get One, at your local CVS and you have multiple MFR BOGO coupons, you could stock up on laundry detergent for the next year, or if you're me—five years. Think of the savings . . . and all the clean clothes!

Note: Keep in mind that if you're using mobile e-coupons as your predominant shopping for free strategy, a lot of the tricks introduced in this chapter (stacking, doubling, and BOGO deals) will be difficult to pull off since you're likely to have only *one* e-coupon per product to play with at a time.

Rain Checks

Many shoppers have no idea that stores issue "rain checks." Do *you* know about this? If a sale item is sold out, most stores will give you a "rain check" to get that item at another time. When the next truck comes in and your item is restocked, you can use your rain check to

HOT TIP: Be Happy for a Rainy Day

Sometimes, getting a rain check is the best thing to happen to an extreme shopper. While you're waiting for your sale item to be restocked, you have time to locate more savings to stack on top of the deal. In other words: Rain checks buy you time.

For example, Target had a sale on Beech-Nut Baby Food for $1.00 and when I got to the store, the shelves were wiped clean (argh!), so I got a rain check for twenty jars—you know me, I buy in bulk. That Sunday, a manufacturer coupon for $1.00 off Beech-Nut food appeared in the inserts. Double score! So, what did I do? I got my hands on twenty of them. When I returned to Target, I used my coupons combined with my rain checks and got all twenty jars for free.   ✂

get the item at its sale price—even if the sale is over. Cool, right? So if you go to CVS to cash in on the Venus Razor BOGO deal and you discover that other shoppers have beat you to it and the shelves are empty, instead of pitching a fit, you can kindly ask a cashier or store manager to give you a rain check. That way, you can return at your leisure and still get the deal while others are back to paying full price. To a competitive shopper like myself, this is simply delayed gratification.

Rebates

I'm a slacker when it comes to mail-in rebates, but I feel like I need to mention them as another smart way to save because so many shoppers I know swear by them. Many manufacturers, and sometimes stores, will offer customers cash back for buying their products. You simply follow the specific instructions on the rebate form, mail it in and they send you a check for cash. My problem is that I always slack off sending in the form before the deadline and if I'd just pick up my own pace, I could save thousands of additional dollars in rebates. I'm not kidding—thousands.

A good girlfriend of mine swears by the Rite Aid rebates. Nearly every week, Rite Aid offers items for free after rebates. They call them "single-check rebates." She uses coupons to buy the items, and then, after rebates, she actually *makes* money. Another shopping buddy of mine regularly takes advantage of the rebate program from Staples. She insists that it's faster and easier than at other stores, and she's gotten calculators, USB chords, and cases of paper for free. Rebates take some diligence and patience, but free is free.

After listening to my friend gloat for months about her Rite Aid rebate earnings and scold me for not jumping into the game, I decided I better at least give it a try. I signed up for the program online and searched for rebate-eligible items to cash in on. (You can pick up their rebate booklet in stores, too.) I made a list, searched my coupon database on www.howtoshopforfree.net for additional savings to slap on top of the deal, and then I hit my nearest Rite Aid. She was right. It's as easy as can be. Thanks to her, I am now making mucho mullah from Rite Aid rebates. Thanks for beating me into submission, girlfriend.

HOT TIP: Submit Once a Month

Rite Aid only allows its customers to submit rebates once a month. You can file more than one rebate per month, but you can only "submit" an online rebate form once a month. So make sure you've cashed in on all the best SCR deals before you hit *SEND ME MY MONEY.* ✂

The first "single-check rebate" deal I worked at Rite Aid was a *Spend $60 on select healthy heart products get a $25.00 gift card*. I did multiple orders to pull this money-maker off.

For my first order, I had a $5 off $20 coupon and so I picked up a Bayer diabetes monitor for $19.99 and another $5 in cereal and juice. I had a high-value coupon to get the monitor free, so after my $5 off $20 coupon, my total bill was zero. Here's the breakdown:

Bayer Monitor	$19.99
Cereal and juice	+ $5.01
TOTAL	= $25.00
$5 off $20 purchase coupon	– $5.00
High value Q for monitor @ $20.00	– $20.00
TOTAL	= FREE

Order number two was very similar. I picked up another Bayer Monitor and combined it with half and half and my favorite dark chocolate for a total of $25. After the $5 off $20 coupon and the coupon for the free monitor, again my total was free.

My last order was a third Bayer Monitor and a pack of Huggies that after coupons, was all free. I registered the three monitors online for a single-check rebate. The total dollars spent was over $60, so Rite Aid rebated me $25. Since my coupons initially took my total down to zero out of pocket (OOP), I made money on this deal. How sweet it is! And what did I do with three diabetes monitors? I donated them to my local senior center.

Truly, the Rite Aid rebate program is a cinch, even for the rebate-challenged like myself. When you buy items that qualify for a single-check rebate (SCR), you simply register your rebate online at www.riteaid.rebateplus.com (Rite Aid does all the math for you), and then (poof) they send you a check or a gift card in the mail. To me, the online process is much easier than fiddling around with a mail-in form.

SHOPPER'S
Hall of Fame

"When I shop at Rite Aid, I concentrate on the items that have a single-check rebate attached to them. I get the items that will come out free using a Rite Aid $5 off $20 coupon combined with Rite Aid store coupons and manufacturer coupons. When I get the SCR in the mail, it's a check that I can deposit in the bank and use for whatever I want. All of those coupons are turned into cash. I've started a separate savings account for my "coupons-to-cash" rebate earnings. There's already $600 in it!"

Charlene, Wells, Maine

Know Your Stores

Holy Mother of Savings! I've given you a lot of information to process. Promise me that you'll sit with it and relax over a latte or one stiff cup of tea before you tear off down the highway to the nearest mini-mall. Remember, it's essential to have a plan together before you set foot in any store, and speaking of that, let's spend some time on the importance of knowing your stores.

Every store is different—how they stock it, staff it, and what their store policy is. For extreme shoppers, these variables are significant. They'll likely determine what stores you want to avoid and those you'll return to again and again.

Store Policy

I've said it before and I'll say it once more: Know your store policy, shoppers. You want to know exactly what kind of deals you can get in every store you shop in. A little education equals more free stuff in your bag.

Find out:

1. What is the store policy on doubling and/or tripling coupons?
2. Does it accept competitor's coupons? (Many do.)
3. How many multiple items are allowed?
4. Does it have a stacking (combining coupons) policy?
5. Does it accept expired coupons? (Believe it or not, some do.)
6. Are there any special conditions for BOGOs?
7. And finally, what's the store's hard line on accepting online printables? Remember: some stores have put the kibosh on this.

Send the store an e-mail message and ask them to send you a copy of their policy, or look it up online. The policy is usually a simple, single sheet and quite conversational, so there's no excuse for not doing your homework. Target's store policy begins with,

> Dear Target Guest, Coupons are a great way to save even more when shopping at Target, and we make it easy to use them at our stores. But because of the variety of coupons available to our guests, we do have some guidelines for how coupons can be redeemed . . .

Friendly, right?

Personally, I like to have a hard copy of the store policy on me when I'm shopping, so I can whip it out and refer to it in the checkout line if need be. I've highlighted the most contentious points for easy reference. (I don't expect you to geek out like I do, but it does come in handy.) Having a copy on you isn't necessary because all cashiers should have a policy at check-out. Some will actually tape it to the counter that the debit machine is on. Even so, cashiers don't always know their own store policy, so it's best to educate yourself so you can educate them.

Staff

Shopping for free is pretty darn exciting, and infectious. You'll be surprised how many cashiers, along with the people standing behind you in line, become your cheerleaders. Young guys are often the best cashiers. I've found that they're either totally disinterested or completely enthusiastic. One of my fondest memories is when a young male cashier asked me for my autograph. "I saw you doing this on TV!" he nearly screamed. I'm still thinking about setting that sweetie-pie up with my nineteen-year-old daughter. Who wouldn't want a son-in-law who appreciates a woman who shops for free?

You'll find that most cashiers are very cool, but I must warn you that once in a while you may be confronted by someone who questions your masterful shopping strategy. Don't let them rattle you (after all, you know the store policy inside and out). In my experience, the cashiers who frown upon super shoppers just don't understand how it works; they cannot wrap their minds around how you're getting a

HOT TIP: Be Nice

Yeah, it's obvious but sometimes we need to be reminded. If you're poised to walk out the door with a bounty of loot you've paid hardly anything for, showing some patience and giving up a little extra nice is worth it, wouldn't you agree? If someone's giving you a fuss, reference the store policy with a friendly grin. Stand your ground with civility and grace. If that doesn't work, ask for the manager. When all else fails, demand they call the corporate office (with a wink and a smile, of course).

cartload of stuff for free, and they think you *must* be cheating the system somehow. Not true: Even when you shop for free, the stores still make money. Remember: Stores get incentives and are reimbursed when customers use coupons, so don't put on the guilty face in the check-out line. You're winning. The store is winning.

Should you find yourself debating legality with a cashier who thinks you're trying to rob the store, inhale, exhale, and calmly explain the store policy to them. When I find myself in situations like this, I take on the role of teacher. I've encountered my share of hesitant cashiers who've given me the "That's-sure-a-lot-of-stuff" look, to which I enthusiastically respond, "I know! And it's going to be FREE after all these coupons. Would you like me to show you how I do it?" If they just don't get it, I school them. Once they catch on to the deals I'm getting, they often want me to help *them* shop for free. Seriously, I've made a lot of friends and allies this way.

Take a Lot, But Don't Hog It All

That's my personal rule, and one I hope you'll adopt. Once you start shopping for free, you may be tempted to take it all. If you can get five boxes of energy-saving light bulbs for nothing, what's stopping you from clearing out the entire stock? Show some self-restraint. Remember your fellow shoppers want to get some, too, so try to always leave something behind. Getting more is always tempting, but greedy. Now, not all coupon junkies believe the same way I do so it's not a bad idea to learn your stores' shipment and delivery schedule. Although you can always get a rain check, it will probably start to grate on you if every time you shop a sale, there's nothing left for you. It's true that a lot of sale items sell out on the first day of a sale, but the next shipment is usually on the way. Plan accordingly.

HOT TIP: Read the Fine Print

In an attempt to control greediness, be fair, and make sure everyone gets what they want, stores will sometimes limit the number of sale items one individual can throw into her basket. If you have any question about limitations, just reference the store ad or read the shelf tag. It will be clearly stated: *Limit 3 per customer*, for example. There's nothing worse than thinking you're getting ten bottles of your favorite nail polish for nothing when the limit is three!

Before we move on to Chapter 4: The Secret to Stockpiling, I want you to promise yourself that you won't try all the savings tricks you've just learned at once. Pick one or two, like working a BOGO deal or doubling a coupon, and play around with them until you're comfortable. Once you've figured out how to make a deal work, add something new into the mix. Remember: slow and steady. My goal is to teach you to shop for free, not make you feel like you have ADHD. ✂

WORK IT: TAKE A FIELD TRIP

Go on a personal field trip mission. Your mission is to find three things that work out for free. I'm convinced that's all it'll take for you to be hooked, and shopping will never be the same for you again.

Go to your favorite grocery, drug store, or large retail store. Take a small notebook, a pen, and your shopping buddy. Scan the aisles for things priced under one to two bucks and write these items down.

After you've jotted down a few things, go home and try to find three coupons for these products in the www.howtoshopforfree.net database or from your personal coupon stash that will make those items free.

I had to do this once when a show producer called me from a local TV station interested in doing a consumer reports story on how I feed my family on four bucks a week. She'd heard I pay for cartloads of groceries with pennies and asked if she could send a TV crew the following day to shoot me in action. I panicked, thinking, *Tomorrow? How am I going to pull this off with such short notice?*

I shook off the anxiety, put on my big girls pants, and took myself on a field trip. I walked up and down the aisles, like I've advised you to do, hunting for free stuff. The first thing I found was my favorite Greek yogurt on sale for a dollar. Score! I knew I had twenty $1-off coupons at home, making twenty of those bad boys free. Then, I spotted Uncle Ben's rice on sale for a $1.00 and Perdue chicken on sale for $2.00. I knew I had coupons at home to make several chicken and rice meals totally free. I quietly scolded myself for my momentary doubt. After all, I can shop for free in my sleep. After that, my field trip became a fun frolic through Freeville. I located what would be free after coupons: cat treats, dog bones, air freshener, dishwashing detergent, dental floss, cereal, Healthy Choice frozen meals, and on and on.

The next day when the TV crew followed me through the store, they were amazed at how quickly my cart filled up—correction: how my *three* carts filled up. My total grocery bill came to $384.00, but after mixing and matching coupons, it totaled five dollars. No joke. I had so much stuff that my four-year-old son was hardly visible in the back seat of my car. In fact, I had to offload several bags to the reporter. Moral of the story: You can have more for less. Believe in free.   ✂

Resources: A Glossary of How to Shop for Free-isms

BOGO: Buy One, Get One

Blinkies: Little red coupon machines in grocery store aisles with small red blinking lights

CAT or Catalina deal: A group of items that when purchased together produce a money-off coupon for a future purchase. The money-off coupon prints out of the Catalina machine that sits next to the cash register.

ESC and ESR: Easy Saver Catalog and Easy Saver Rebate available at Walgreens.

ECBs: Extra Care Bucks (CVS)

FAR: Free after rebate

GM: General Mills

IP: Internet printable

ISO: In search of

MFR: Manufacturer

MFR Q or MQ: Manufacturer coupon

MIR: Mail in rebate

OOP: Out of pocket

OYNO: On your next order

Peelies: Coupons you find on the product itself and you peel off

PG: Procter & Gamble

PSP: Pre-sale price

Q: Coupon

RA: Rite Aid

RAOK: Random act of kindness

RP: RedPlum, a Sunday coupon insert

RR: Register Reward (Walgreens)

SCR: Single-check rebate (Rite Aid)

SS: SmartSource, a Sunday coupon insert

Tear pads: A block of coupons from which you tear off individual coupons

Wags: Walgreens

Wine tag: A coupon that hangs on a bottle of wine. Some say "no wine purchase necessary" and are often redeemable for fresh fruit and meat.

WYB: When you buy

YMMV: Your mileage may vary

4

The Secret to Stockpiling

My personal philosophy is that if I can get something for free, I'm going to get as many of those free items as possible. Girls, this is nothing to feel guilty or little piggy-ish about. Great deals don't stay on the shelves forever, so if I can get my favorite party crackers for free for a limited time, I take my fair share. Nothing beats the rush of loading your cart full and knowing that you won't be paying a penny for it. I'm used to people questioning this logic. They say, "Kathy, why do you need twenty boxes of Wheat Thins?" Because eventually I will use them. Or I will give them away to someone who will.

What's in the cart?

Here's what you'll find in this chapter:
- The difference between hoarding and stockpiling
- The best products to stockpile
- How your stockpile determines your menu du jour
- Storage tips, including how to stockpile in a studio apartment

Stockpiling—*Not* Hoarding

If you want to shop for free, stockpiling, after organization, is key. Stockpiling is simply a shopping strategy. When a product you regularly use goes on sale and/or you can get it for free by combining coupons with sales, you snatch up as many of those items as you can. Your ultimate goal will be to replace everything you need before you run out, so that you're never paying top dollar again. For example, the last time I checked, I counted forty-five tubes of toothpaste in my bathroom cabinet that I paid nothing for. Because I found a way to work a toothpaste deal for free, I stocked up heavily on my favorite whitening gel. Toothpaste is one of those ideal household items to stockpile because it doesn't go bad, and you always need it (especially in my household of six). *And*, purchased individually, it's not cheap.

Readers, I realize that to many of you, I sound like a shopping fanatic, and maybe certifiably loony-tunes. Let me assure you that I don't spend *all* my time dreaming up coupon capers. I also garden, cook, do art projects with my kids, and volunteer my time at the local senior center. But let's get back to my passion: shopping.

I regularly teach classes to women on how to shop for free and at the mention of stockpiling, I'm always met with one or two uncomfortable glances from the group. I get it. The idea of buying, or free-loading, more than one needs seems greedy, unnecessary, paranoid, and gluttonous. With that unflattering image in mind, let me set the record straight. I'm familiar with the TV show *Hoarders*, where unassuming suburbanites have stacked their homes floor to ceiling with so much stuff they can't find their own toilet. That is not the kind of compulsive behavior I'm encouraging here. What I *am* suggesting is that when you find a good deal on something you use often, buy as much of it as you can.

When you stock up on your favorite repeat items, you shorten your shopping list for weeks, and sometimes months to come, and most importantly, you save money. Not buying it? Let me ask you this: What's the average price for a box of cereal these days? Around four bucks, right? I don't know about you, but the idea of spending that kind of money on something that's gone practically before the box is opened puts me in a nasty mood. Thankfully, I've figured out how, after discounts and coupons, to get cereal for practically nothing. When I'm splurging, I'll spend, *at most*, fifty cents on my favorite granola. At this bargain price, I buy ten at a time. My family is set for weeks and if I've spent anything at all, it's hardly more than the cost of *one* box. When I explain this type of stockpiling scenario in my workshops, a nervous voice always makes the point—But, you don't need ten boxes at one time. True. But eventually, my family and I will make good use of each and every one of those ten boxes. So if I can get a great deal on ten, I'll buy ten and stash them away. If you figure the average cereal-eating household inhales one box per week, most families will buy over fifty boxes a year. If you can get a killer deal today, stock up now, and save yourself time later on and, most importantly, a sizable amount of cash.

I've been shopping this way for a while, so it makes perfect sense to me. It might take you some time to get used to the idea of buying twenty boxes of penne pasta in one go, but I think eventually, you'll feel a sense of relief knowing that your pantry, bathroom drawers, and laundry room shelves are always stocked (I know I do). Because I stockpile, there are often weeks when I don't shop at all: I've done such an excellent job stockpiling deals that I have everything I need. *Imagine that—having everything you need.*

 You Asked It

Q: I'm single and live in a small apartment. Not only do I have limited space, but I can't think of much that I need to buy multiples of. Maybe I'm not a good candidate for stockpiling?

A: Buying in bulk is one thing, deciding where to put it is another. I'll give you some solid ideas on what to do with all that stuff a little later in the chapter. As to whether stockpiling is relevant to someone who is single or living with just one or two people, the answer is Yes—absolutely. No matter the size of your household, there are plenty of products worth stockpiling. (If you're living alone, twenty boxes of pasta might be a little excessive. Try ten. And if you have a gluten allergy, stockpiling pasta won't be your thing. Only you know what your specific tastes and space will allow for.)

Just to give you an idea of popular food items that you could start stockpiling for free, or nearly free, on your next shopping trip, take a look below. I'm guessing many of these items appear regularly on your shopping list, and, as a general rule, you pay top dollar for them. Think about it: If you can get everything on this list for free, or nearly free, why not stock up for months and save yourself some time and money?

Staples

- Olive oil
- Butter
- Mayo
- Mustard
- Ketchup
- Tomato paste
- Chicken stock
- Bread crumbs
- BBQ sauce
- Hot sauce
- Salad dressing
- Sugar
- Salt
- Seasonings

Non-Perishables

- Soups
- Canned vegetables
- Canned beans
- Tuna fish
- Pasta sauce
- Pasta noodles
- Peanut butter
- Jams and jellies
- Bottled water
- Seltzer water
- Juice

Perishables
(If you can freeze it,
you can stockpile it.)
- Bread and tortillas
- Meat
- Seafood
- Shredded cheese
- Frozen meals

Cleaning supplies
- Air freshener
- Laundry detergent
- Dishwashing detergent
- Dish soap

Toiletries
- Toilet paper
- Facial tissue
- Toothpaste
- Dental floss
- Contact lens solution
- Body wash
- Deodorant
- Tampons
- Soap
- Razors
- Shaving cream
- Q-tips
- Cotton balls

Pretty impressive list, isn't it? If it's something that won't go bad or expire, then I say—get it. You will use it. (And in case you're wondering, I'll tell you how you can extend the life of your perishables—stay tuned for that).

Still not convinced that you consume or use enough of any one item to stockpile it? If so, here's a challenge for you.

WORK IT: DO THE MATH ON YOUR CONSUMPTION

The next time you open a bottle or container of something you consume regularly, whip out your magic marker and write the date on the container. If it's peanut butter, write the date you crack the seal on the side of the jar. After you've emptied it of all its nutty, salty goodness, note the date. If it took you three weeks to go through it, then you'll know that a six-month stockpile of peanut butter equals eight jars (yes, more math). If you're eventually going to buy eight jars, save yourself some time and money by jumping on the first saltilicious peanut butter deal you come across. Buy eight jars, stash them away, and then forget about it!

If you happen to be someone with kids in the house, I probably don't have to convince you of the merits of stockpiling, but should you need that extra jolt of motivation, here it is: Stockpiling will save you hundreds of trips to the store (and probably some much-deserved sanity). I stockpile energy bars, chips, cookies, pretzels, and nuts, and it's saved me from going totally ballistic when my kids whine, "Mom, I'm starving. There's nothing in the house to eat." I calmly point them in the direction of our pantry stocked with family-friendly goodies and count backward from ten.   ✂

You Asked It

Q: *It seems like coupons are only for processed junk foods. Is that true? I don't want to stockpile "junk."*

A: *From time to time, I meet groups of women to show them how I shop for free. I can't tell you how often I've been greeted in public with something like, "You're Kathy? I thought you'd be heavier and more grandmotherly."* Translation: fat and nearly dead. *Seriously, women have said this to my face. Not only have people been surprised to learn that I'm not overweight, but they're confused when they realize my kids aren't either. News flash: Not all deals apply to junk food or crap that's heavily processed, full of high fructose corn syrup and sodium. While it's true that I appeared on national television showing off the twenty-one bags of Double Stuff Oreos stockpiled in my pantry, I regularly have rows and rows of Healthy Choice soup cans lining the shelves and countless organic food items in my refrigerator. True, there are A LOT of coupons for junky foods that come in a box, but there are just as many coupons for healthy foods, too. (Don't believe me? Hold your breath: There's more on shopping for meat, produce, dairy, and organic for free in Chapter 8.)*

Make a List

To put you in the stockpiling mindset, take a look around your kitchen, laundry room, and bathroom and start a list of non-perishable items you replace often. For each item on your list, guesstimate how many you will need for the next six to twelve months. *Not sure?* This is where marking the box, bag, or jar with the date you open comes in handy—trust me, it really will help you keep track. You can also start an inventory list of non-perishable items and keep notes on when you bought them and when they ran out. You will soon become aware of what household items you're frequently spending money on. These are the items to begin stockpiling.

Checklist
Stockpiling

✓ Start with two to three items to stockpile
✓ Look for in-store deals on your item
✓ Look for MFR coupons to stack on top of a sale
✓ Stock up

HOT TIP: Go Straight to the Source

If you want to stockpile something brand-specific, like Pillsbury All-Purpose Flour, in addition to checking the database at www.howtoshopforfree.net, go straight to the manufacturer website and see what kind of coupons are available. Often you can print coupons directly from an MFR site and sometimes even score exclusive discounts for going straight to the source.

Once you've designated two to three items to shop for, begin scanning the weekly circulars, either online or in the paper, and look for opportunities to stockpile your item. Let's say you do a lot of baking and you quickly go through bags of flour. Consider this one of your first items to stockpile. If, for example, you notice that your local grocery store is having a sale on Pillsbury All-Purpose flour, search the coupon database at www.howtoshopforfree.net for a coupon you can match with the sale. If you can save significantly on one bag, buy five or ten. Stock up! This will save you money and time in the long run.

Shop Around

I shop around because there are countless deals to be had, and I don't want to miss out on any of them. Sometimes fantastic deals aren't always advertised, either. It's those little known deals you want to scoop up. Most shoppers are store-loyal and, as a result, often pay more for items that are selling for a whole lot less just down the street. Not you. Not anymore.

I've memorized the prices for a whole mixed bag of items all up and down the North Shore, so when high-value coupons are issued for products I like, I automatically know which stores will give me the best bang for my buck. For example, I know that Market Basket usually sells Marcal toilet paper 4-paks for a buck, so when $1.00-off Marcal coupons come out (and they do with fantastic frequency), I know exactly where to stockpile toilet paper for free.

Don't worry, I won't ask you to commit all your stores' prices to memory, but what I would like you to do is to begin to notice the prices for items you normally buy in the different stores you shop in. You *are* shopping in multiple stores now, right? You may be surprised at the price discrepancy between stores. For example, one of my more health-conscious members discovered that Omega-3 cage free eggs at a natural grocer in her area were always cheaper (as in 99 cents cheaper) than the regular eggs in all the other stores in her area. For whatever reason, her natural grocer didn't advertise this awesome egg deal, so she wouldn't have known about it had she not been in the store scoring heavily on discounted vitamins one afternoon.

Once you become comfortable mixing and matching sales with coupons, start comparison-shopping. You don't need to go crazy with this. I know a lot of hard-core shoppers out there who like to record prices from different stores in an actual price book, but I don't think this is necessary. Already with your shopping list, personal number to beat, and stash of coupons, you're juggling a lot. No need to over-do it. Just make mental notes or, if you think you won't remember, jot prices down on your shopping list as you cruise the aisles. For example, if turkey chili is a favorite of yours to make, take note of the price of ground turkey in different stores. Once you determine the store that offers it at the lowest price, wait for it to go on sale, be ready to apply MFR coupons to the deal (Jennie-O coupons are always easy to come by), and then stock up. Buy as much as you can and throw it right into your freezer.

HOT TIP: Geek Out

For those of you who think comparison-shopping sounds laborious and too time-consuming, then check this out: Barcode apps like ShopSavvy (www.biggu.com/) and RedLaser (www.redlaser.com) allow you to scan product barcodes right there in the store aisles using your Android-based phone or iPhone, respectively. Once the code is identified, you're provided with competing prices in local stores and online. This is pretty cool technology but take it from me—overly caffeinated or harried shoppers will find it hard to hold the phone steady long enough for the code to scan. ✂

You Asked It

Q: *If stockpiling is key, wouldn't buying in bulk at a wholesale club be the better way to go?*

A: *There's a difference between buying in bulk and stockpiling. I buy single items that I can stockpile versus buying bulk packages from a warehouse store. Here's why: I can knock the price down much lower on a single item than on a discounted bundled package. For example, Near East rice pilaf usually goes for $2.99 a box. That's $35.88 for twelve boxes. If the nearest wholesale club is selling a 12-pack of Near East rice pilaf at a discounted price of $29.37, I bet you'd be inclined to cash in on this deal. But, hold on. If your local grocery store is running a special on Near East rice pilaf, two boxes for $3, what's the better deal?*

12-pack of Near East Rice Pilaf full retail price	= $35.88
Wholesale club discounted price	= $29.37
Local grocer 12 boxes @ 2 for $3.00	= $18.00

It's more cost efficient to buy individual boxes versus a discounted bundle. What's more, if you had a stack of $0.75-off/1 box coupons that doubled to $1.50 off, your total cost for 12 boxes would be zero, zip, nada.

Local grocer 12 boxes @ 2 for $3.00	= $18.00
Coupons $0.75 off, doubled to $1.50 x 12	− $18.00
TOTAL	= FREE

That's right—twelve boxes for nothing. In a situation like this, I clear the shelves. Correction: I nearly clear the shelves. It's not polite to take it all.

Wholesale clubs make a lot of sense for many people, so I'm not suggesting you cancel your membership. They can be very convenient and the free food samples are a tasty perk. Also, buying in bulk often lowers the per unit price, and that saves you money. It's just that you won't ever shop for free at a wholesale club. The only exception to this rule is that some (not all) wholesale clubs will let you use coupons on individually wrapped items within the bulk package. So for example, if you're buying a package of twenty tubes of toothpaste, you might be able to use twenty MFR coupons, one for each tube, bringing your already discounted cost down even lower. But why do that when you can score free tubes of toothpaste at pharmacies and supermarket chains on any given day?

Don't Let the Numbers Fool You

There's a huge population of shoppers out there who will tell you that the smartest way to shop is by comparing unit prices. I disagree. Here's why: Let's say you're looking for the best deal on cat food. You scan the aisles and find a 17-pound bag that costs $0.39 per pound compared to a 3-pound bag at $1.29 per pound. What's the better deal? Thirty-nine cents is the lowest price per pound, so that's the one to get, right? Wrong.

Coupons turn this logic upside down. Here's how I work it:

A 3-pound bag of Iams cat food is a pricey $1.29 per pound. One 3-pound bag costs me $3.87. But because I have ten coupons for $4.00 off *any* Iams cat food, I buy ten bags and score 30 pounds of cat food for free. Free trumps a low unit price any day, wouldn't you agree?

HOT TIP: Buy Small, Save Big

Always try to apply coupons to the least expensive (and this usually means smaller) bag/box/can of the products you buy regularly. In many cases, it'll work out free, or nearly free. Use multiple coupons to get multiples of this item and stockpile.   ✂

Don't Let the Brand Fool You

I've already said my piece about brand loyalty, so I won't repeat myself, but let me also add that buying generic products is not cheaper than buying name brands. In general, buying generic brands over name brands is the more cost-efficient way to go, but you'll be hard-pressed to find coupons for generic brands. Coupons for name-brand products, however, are practically falling from the store ceilings. It's the big players—Kraft, General Mills, Procter & Gamble, Betty Crocker—that issue the majority of coupons, so if you're shopping for free, it's nearly impossible to walk out of the store *without* top name brands.

How Much Is Too Much?

To give you an idea of what I might stockpile in a week, check out the items below that I pulled from an old receipt. Remember, I have kids in the house who will murder me in my sleep if I don't bring home a moderate amount of junk food; one woman's stockpile may indeed be another woman's hoard. You'll quickly learn what works for you and your family.

- **50 boxes of Cheese Nips.** On sale for $0.99 apiece. I used $1.00 off MFR coupons making them all free. I made five trips to pull this caper off.
- **30 José Olé burritos.** On sale for $0.99 a box. They were part of a deal such that when you buy ten frozen items you get $10.00 off your next order (OYNO). I bought ten burritos, got ten bucks back, rolled that cash into my next order of ten burritos and so on. All free.
- **40 containers of Wholly Guacamole.** Free with a "Try Me" promotional coupon. Inhaled two containers when I got home and froze the rest.
- **10 boxes of PureVia sugar.** On sale for $2.00 a box. I used MFR coupons for $2.00 off, making them all free.
- **20 rolls of Marcal paper towels.** On sale for $0.99 a roll. I used MFR coupons for $1.00 off, making them all free.
- **20 bags of Purina cat food.** On sale for $2.39 a bag. I used $3.00 off any bag, making them all free.

Holy guacamole, is right! I realize this is a massive amount of stuff, so I just want to reiterate: Hoarding isn't my thing. Really. While it's true that if I can get something for free, I get as much as I can, what my family doesn't use, I give away.

The Shopping High

Definition: A rushing feeling described by light-headedness, an elevated heart rate, including the uncontrollable urge to yell, "WOO HOO!" Severe cases include the compulsion to call friends and loved ones and announce, "Oh my Gawd. You won't believe what I just paid for a cartload of stuff! A dime. A freakin' dime!"

I'm not going to lie—the free shopping high is real. And once you figure out how to stockpile, watch out! I've been with women who, when they realized they could get multiples of a favorite product for free, involuntarily peed in their pants from all the excitement. (BTW: adult diapers are always free.) I've seen shoppers break out in heated sweats and heard admissions, like "Shopping is better than sex" and "I need more." There's no telling how shopping for free will affect you, so in the weeks and months ahead, simply keep yourself

HOT TIP: Share More than You Keep

In Chapter 12: Pay It Forward, I go deep into the importance of charitable acts. Simply, I share with those who don't shop like I do and, for whatever reason, need help. This could be a neighbor, a friend of the family, a shut-in, the nearby food pantry, women's shelter, or senior center. Giving to the less fortunate feels amazing. It's better than any shopping high.   ✂

in check. Should you notice your shopping becoming more feverish and frantic, rest assured that free deals never run out. Truly, I could shop 24/7 and always find a deal. So relax. You can get your fix whenever you need it.

Don't think crazy shopper can happen to you? In that case, I guess I have to reveal one of my dirty little secrets: guarding products. It was just an ordinary day in CVS. I was shopping with my kids in tow when I turned the corner and right there on the clearance shelf was clumping cat litter. It was marked down to $0.69 a jug container. Clumping cat litter, which regularly retails at $6.99 or so, is not an easy item to score for close to nothing. My heart started pounding and I yelled at my kids, "Go get a carriage! HURRY!" They saw the crazy in my eyes, and they ran.

While they were off retrieving Mommy her precious shopping cart, I stood guarding that clumping cat litter with my life. I'm fairly certain that had another shopper threatened to touch my litter—all ten of those 69-cent jugs were MINE—things would've gotten ugly. It was only after we were back in the car with every last one that I thought, *Maybe I just crossed a line?*

You Asked It

Q: *How do most stores feel about shoppers stockpiling? Wouldn't they try to stop one shopper from clearing a whole shelf, especially when she uses coupons to get it all for nothing?*

A: *The bottom line is that stores want to make money. If one shopper wipes out an entire shelf of sale items and uses coupons to do it, the store still makes a profit. Remember: The manufacturer reimburses the store for every coupon redeemed. That said, most stores don't want to run out of their hottest advertised sale items before their promotional window closes. So if you know ahead of time that you'll be grabbing up double armloads of an upcoming sale item, let the store know. I've found they appreciate the heads-up, and they're often very cool about it. In fact, many stores will go so far as to put in a special order for you. Feeling shy? Don't be afraid to ask. Here are three conversations to pick from, depending on your level of comfort.*

1. *You (savvy shopper) approach the service desk: "I see that you are having a great deal on soup next week and I would really love to stock up, but I'm afraid everyone else will be doing the same thing. Is there anyone that could order extra or is there any way I could have a case of it put aside for me?"*

2. *You (killer shopper) call the service desk: "Hi, can I speak to the store manager or the stock manager please? I see that next week you are having a sale on Wheat Thins for $2.00. I would like to purchase 40 boxes. Is it possible to ask for you to order extra stock and hold them for me until Wednesday? Should I ask to see you when I come in or will they be waiting for me at the service desk?"*

3. *You (hard-core, extreme shopper) call the service desk: "Yes, can I talk to Drew, the stock manager. Hi Drew, can you grab next week's ad. See the Hunts ketchup, Orville Redenbacher popcorn, Breyers ice cream, and fruit roll ups that are in the "deals" on the back page? Well, they are going to sell off the shelf faster than you can possibly stock them. It's a killer CAT week. (CATalina deals to be discussed in Chapter 8.) All of the coupon divas will be there. Can you give me a call when the truck comes in? You need to order at least an extra 500 Hunts ketchup to keep up with the demand and can you put 60 aside for me? I will also take anything that's left over on the last day of the sale so don't worry. You really can't over order."*

When the cashiers at my local grocery stores see me coming, they open up a separate checkout lane. They know I mean business.

Where to Put All That Stuff

Of course, you're going to get home with your 20 bags of cat food, 50 rolls of toilet paper, and 90 cans of tuna fish and think, "Where on earth am I going put all of this?" I live in a suburban-style home, so I've got all my closets, cabinets, attic, and basement full, and when it comes to perishables, I freeze just about everything.

Depending on how much cabinet and closet space you have, I suggest aiming to stockpile a year's worth of non-perishables. It's amazing how much you can stash away once you re-organize your existing space. I stockpile for five years, but you know me. I'm in my own category of "shopping freak."

Before you start stockpiling for the months ahead, I suggest doing the following:

- Take an inventory of your living space. Are there any closets or cabinets that could be better organized to make room for all the free loot you're about to start bringing home?
- Start by designating one space for your stockpile. When that fills up, find another.
- See where you can condense or combine cabinets before adding stand-alone storage units.
- Join the ongoing forum discussion "How to Organize Your Stash" on www.howtoshopforfree.net. You're sure to find many creative solutions.

My kitchen pantry—which I had custom built for my stockpile—is three feet deep and eight feet high and looks not unlike a supermarket shelf. Products like cooking oils, salad dressing, and condiments are grouped together on one shelf. Starches like cereal, breakfast bars, crackers, and chips are on another. My tomato paste, pinto beans, and soup cans are stacked two tall and eight deep with their labels facing forward. Sure, it's a little OCD, but

I always know what I have on hand, and it's kind of fun shopping in your own home.

Expiration Dates

A full cabinet is only good if the contents in it haven't gone bad. Even non-perishables eventually take a turn for the worse, so get in the habit of rotating your stock. About twice a month, I move cans, bottles and boxes from the back of my pantry shelves to the front so I'm always rotating out the oldest products versus the stuff I brought home yesterday. If I notice that I've overstocked something that's likely to go south before my family will use it, I give it away.

When my pantry becomes stuffed to capacity, I take my stockpile downstairs to the basement. I have a large plastic shelving unit down there where I store my overflow non-perishable foods and my cleaning supplies like laundry detergent and dishwashing soap. Next to that storage unit is my deep freezer. This is where I store most of our meat, cheeses, breads, frozen foods, and ice cream. (Again, depending on

---

SHOPPER'S
Hall of Fame

"You may be turned off by the idea of stockpiling, but it is completely worth it. Having a stockpile of items you have received free, or close to it, is much better than running out of an essential item and having to make a trip to the store to pay full price. The key to stockpiling is organization. You just need to dedicate a spot in your house for organizing all of your free stuff. I am one of those people who have very limited space, but I have huge stockpiles hidden. For example, I have two shelving units in my house that are simple, cheap, and designed to look like bookshelves."

Michelle, Waterloo, Illinois

HOT TIP: Strip It Down

Many frozen packaged foods come well wrapped inside the box, so to maximize space in the freezer, remove your veggie burgers, chicken pot pies, rice bowls, and breakfast burritos from their bulky boxes. My kids are waffle fanatics, so to keep their favorite breakfast food in stock, I recycle the boxes and stack the individually wrapped waffles one on top of each other in the freezer.   ✂

your available space, I recommend stockpiling six months' worth of perishables.) I always know what's in my downstairs freezer and when it went in because I circle the expiration date on the package before throwing it into the deep freeze, and every couple of weeks, I rotate my inventory. Even in a freezer, food will eventually go bad, so rotate your stockpile. What's the point of stocking up on all your favorite foods if you're just going to let them freeze to death?

Checklist
Deep Freezing

- ✓ Rotate your meat. Generally, meat is good for six months, although I've pulled hamburger out at the eight-month mark and everyone's still alive. Use your best judgment.
- ✓ Divide big pieces of pork, chicken, and beef into smaller orders sealed in individual freezer bags. (Don't forget to date them.)
- ✓ Pull out just enough of what you need without wasting valuable protein. Cook to order.

SHOPPER'S
Hall of Fame

"As amazing as it is getting deals, it is NOTHING compared to squeezing that last bit out of the toothpaste tube or taking the last roll of toilet paper out of the closet and not having that sinking feeling of 'Oh great, now I have to go to the store tomorrow,' but instead thinking 'Oh, I have to grab a tube/roll next time I am downstairs switching laundry.' Nothing beats the feeling of knowing you HAVE it . . . no running out, no paying full price."

Christie, Middletown, Maryland

Meal Planning

It takes a while to fully stock a house. It's not like one shopping trip will transform your cupboards into something resembling the pantry on *Top Chef*. So if you're someone who likes to eat *what* you want to eat *when* you want to eat it, what I'm going to say next might upset your stomach: Let what works out for free, or nearly free, determine your meal plan. In my house, my husband refers to the SmartSource insert as his "menu." Every Sunday after I've perused the inserts and cross-checked savings with upcoming grocery deals, he'll ask, "What's for dinner this week?" If, for example, after matching coupons with a store sale, taco shells will work out free, I know I'll be whipping up a Mexican feast the following week. I almost always have a stockpile of beans, salsa, guacamole, shredded cheese, and chicken on hand, so taco night is an easy one to pull off. When you let sales, along with your stockpile, guide what foods you prepare, you'll start to see your grocery bills shrink considerably. This doesn't mean you can't eat what you want when you want it. Just know it'll cost you more.

Stockpiling in a Studio Apartment

No matter how little or how much space you have, you'll find that stockpiling provides you with an excellent opportunity to get organized. With that much loot, you kind of have to be. If you live in a studio or a small city apartment and your living space is already cramped, consider the following storage ideas that will help you take advantage of the longer-term deals that you're sure to find.

- Utilize the kitchen. In most studios, the kitchen gives you the most real estate. If you have decent counter space, think about storing your dishware on the counter top and stockpile your cabinets. (Even with a fairly spacious kitchen, I keep all my cooking utensils in decorative jars so I can stuff my drawers.) If you have surface space above your cabinets, store additional items there.
- Stash your stock in stackable boxes. Invest in decorative storage boxes to minimize the "still-unpacking" and "living-out-of-a-box" look.
- Check for alcoves. Usually you can find an odd segment of wall that could fit a storage piece from IKEA.
- Build up. Add shelving units above your bed, toilet, and dresser.
- If you have more than one closet, dedicate one to clothes, shoes, and accessories and the other for stockpiling.
- Don't be afraid to get under the bed. Stashing cinnamon buns under your bed might seem a bit unappetizing, but inedible freebies like toilet paper and cleaning supplies can be stashed there indefinitely.
- Take pet food out of the bag. Invest in a plastic storage container on wheels and pour all of your pet's grub into it. Minimizing bags maximizes space and when it's on wheels, you can move it around to wherever you have space.

SHOPPER'S
Hall of Fame

"I'm fairly new to couponing and stockpiling, but I have the non-grocery part of that down. Storage space, well, we are a family of five in a 1400-sq.-ft. house. There is not a lot of room for us to stockpile much. At one point I was keeping things above my washer and dryer, but I soon ran out of the little bit of space I had there. As I was trying to figure out something for storage, it dawned on me that I had an old dresser in my garage. It has worked great to store toothpaste/brushes, shampoo, soap, deodorant, etc. I'm not sure what I will do for storage when that fills up, but I'm sure I can find a few things to get rid of. (Who needs all those tools in the garage?)"

Jennifer, Lowell, Arizona

WORK IT: GROW YOUR STASH

After you've successfully stockpiled two or three products that you use all the time, add another item to your list that you can get for free, or nearly free. Household items like Band-Aids, batteries, razors, toothpaste, toilet paper, and soap can always be found for free. Same goes for kitchen staples like pasta and rice. Every time you shop, aim to grow your stash, even if it's just by a few items. I think you'll be surprised how quickly it adds up. Initially, you may resist spending even a nominal amount of cash for items you don't need *right now*, but trust me, in just a few months, your shopping list will be much shorter than it once was. What's more, your out-of-pocket costs will be significantly lower. Except for perishables, like fresh fruit and veggies, you'll find that you have most everything else you need already put away at home.

5

Like Getting Paid to Shop

Now that you understand the stockpiling philosophy and have been schooled on how to stash all your favorite food items in little nooks and crannies throughout your living space, I want to introduce you to another sure-fire way to get more for less.

Awards programs are one of the quickest ways to start saving even more money. For example, CVS Pharmacy promotes their best weekly Extra Care deals this way: It's like getting it for FREE—and they're not kidding. Many stores have some sort of reward program where you get cash back, or store credit, for buying promoted items. I have loyalty and reward cards for a variety of stores peddling makeup, home furnishings, office materials, pet supplies, and books. In many cases, you get the same amount of money back that you spent in the first place. This might not seem like a very good business plan, but let's not spend our time worrying about that. Let's get shopping.

What's in the cart?

Here's what you'll find in this chapter:

- How each program works

- How to save even more when you use my "hot tips" and shopping strategies
- How to cash in on unique savings opportunities at the mall
- How to work deals from the gym to the gas pump

Pharmacies

CVS — The CVS program is a great one to start with. It's easy to sign up, and you'll see savings immediately. You will need to make an initial investment, but if you plan wisely, you'll potentially never have to spend real money in CVS again. Four years ago, I spent eight bucks when I signed up for the CVS Extra Care Program, and that's all I've spent in that store since. (And I shop there a lot.)

Before you can begin saving, you'll need an Extra Care Card. This is a rewards card, not a store credit card. You can sign up for one online, or ask for one in the store. I recommend signing up in a CVS store, so you can start using it pronto. Be sure to register the card online, too, and you'll receive a high-value welcome coupon, and e-mail alerts about red-hot deals will start appearing in your inbox.

As soon as you get your card, use it every time you make a purchase at CVS. Here's why: The card shaves money off nearly every purchase you make and allows you to earn Extra Care Bucks (ECBs) when you buy designated items. What's an Extra Care Buck? It's like a regular buck. As in, cash.

For example, say CVS has a deal on Coca-Cola products. Buy three 12-packs for $10, earn $3 in ECBs.

You fork out an initial ten bucks, but you get three back in ECBs. So really, you're getting three 12-packs for seven bucks. You follow? The $3 you get back in ECBs, you get to spend on your next shopping trip just like regular money. *Note:* ECBs work as cash, but they don't look like cash. Your Extra Bucks print out at the bottom of your receipt, so don't throw your receipts away!

If you ask me, ECBs are a shopper's best friend. They can be used on practically every item in the store, and new opportunities to earn them change week to week. New deals are published on Sunday, so check your local CVS circular online or pick one up at the store, then bust out your favorite magic marker and circle everything that will reward you with ECBs the following week. The savings quickly add up and, at the end of each quarter (every three months), you'll be rewarded with 2 percent back on all purchases made at CVS. Seriously, you can't go wrong with this program.

Maybe you're thinking, I get how they work, but I don't understand why Kathy hasn't had to spend any "real" money in CVS for the past four years. Good catch! The best ECB deals are the ones where you get back the same dollar amount you spend. For example, say you purchase a bottle of Newman's Own Pasta Sauce that's on sale for $1.99 and the store gives you $1.99 back in ECBs—it's free.

Newman's Own Pasta Sauce	$1.99
Your out of pocket costs	$1.99
ECBs Back	+ $1.99
TOTAL	= FREE

You've spent $1.99 out of pocket, but the store has given you your money back in Extra Bucks to use toward your next purchase. The way to really work CVS is to shop *only* for the items that will give you ECBs in return. If you only use your ECBs to make purchases, you won't be spending any real money. This is what we call "rolling" credits, and this is how I've shopped at CVS for four years for free.

WORK IT: LEARN HOW TO ROLL

Once you've earned a fistful of ECBs and rolled a few deals, I want to challenge you to take your shopping game to the next level. At CVS, you can use manufacturer coupons to stack on top of an ECB deal. For example, if you were to pay for the $1.99 Newman's Own Pasta Sauce with manufacturer coupons, then not only would you earn ECBs, you'd actually make money. Check it out:

Newman's Own Pasta Sauce	$1.99
MFR coupon	$0.75 off/1
TOTAL	= $1.24 out of pocket (OOP)
Extra Bucks Back	+ $1.99
	$0.75 Money Maker!

Pretty awesome, right? If only you had more manufacturer coupons for up to $1.99 on any Newman's Own Pasta Sauce, you could make a killing. Imagine how much zesty, low-calorie tomato sauce you could get for nothing. Unfortunately, CVS puts a limit on how many deals one girl can get her hands on, so before you load up your cart with ten bottles of pasta sauce, check the fine print on the shelf tag. Many times, it'll say Extra Bucks offer limit of 1 per household with card. A bit disappointing, yes, but don't pout. There are many more awesome ways to *work it* at CVS and fill up your cart.   ✄

WORK IT: WORK IT SOME MORE AT CVS

Red Price Scanners: Look for the bright red price scanners in your local CVS. When you scan your card, it spits out personalized coupons. Ta-Da! And if you find yourself making a return trip to CVS within the same day, scan your card again. What most shoppers don't know is that you can scan your CVS card multiple times a day before the red light scanner screen asks you to "Try again tomorrow."

HOT TIP: Find Travel Size Deals

Most stores have a travel size section with items priced at a dollar or under. If you have manufacturer coupons for $1 off, then whatever you pick up—shampoo, mouthwash, toothpaste, lotion—it's free. For example, I have a *Spend $20, Get $5* coupon. I buy fifteen travel-size items, use fifteen $1-off/1 coupons and spend five dollars on items I don't have coupons for but need on a regular basis, like eggs or orange juice. After it's all bought and paid for, it's actually free.

Spend $20, Get $5

15 travel size items @ $1 a piece	$15.00
Eggs and OJ	$5.00
TOTAL	$20.00
Use your $5-off $20 coupon	= $15.00
15 MFR coupons @ $1-off	− $15.00
TOTAL	= FREE

Note: If your coupon says, "Not valid on trial sizes" or mentions a size restriction, you can't work this travel size deal. ✄

CVS Rain Checks: Get in the habit of asking for rain checks at CVS. If a sale item is wiped clean from the shelves, not only will CVS give you a rain check to get it at a later date at the sale price, they will also give you the ECBs attached to the deal.

GreenBagTag: Sign up for this reusable bag program for one dollar. CVS will give you a GreenBagTag to attach to your favorite eco-friendly reusable bag. Every time you forego plastic to bag your own stuff, have the cashier scan your GreenBagTag. On every fourth scan, you'll be rewarded with a $1 ECB. It pays to go green.

Reinventing Beauty: Pick up this CVS publication for one dollar. It's packed with high-value coupons redeemable at CVS. Find it in the magazine aisle or displayed near cosmetics.

Money-off coupons: These are advertised in-store and in the weekly CVS circulars. Sometimes they're product-specific and other times they apply to any item in the store.   ✂

Here's an example: Spend $20, Get $8 Extra Bucks when you buy ANY Covergirl Cosmetics. To work this deal, combine MFR Covergirl coupons, store coupons, and ECBs to break even.

If Covergirl Simply Ageless Foundation is selling for $10.99, buy two and spend $21.98. Use two $6.00-off Covergirl Simply Ageless MFR coupons, two $1.00-off any Covergirl product CVS coupons, and $8 Extra Bucks, and break even. Say what? Here's what it looks like:

Buy two @ $10.99 each	$21.98
Use two $6.00-off MFR coupons	– $12.00
Use two $1.00-off store coupons	– $2.00
TOTAL DUE	$7.98
Use Extra Bucks (from previous deals)	– $8.00
OUT OF POCKET =	ZERO
Receive ECBs (for this transaction)	+ $8.00
BREAK EVEN!	

Walgreens — Walgreens, commonly referred to as "Wags" by women who shop for free, has an awards program similar to CVS: When you buy designated items at the store sale price, Walgreens will give you a portion, or *all*, of your money back in "register rewards." *Unlike*

CVS, at Walgreens you do not need to sign up for a store loyalty program to cash in on their weekly deals. Register rewards, or RRs as we say in the shopping biz, print out at the register and say something like, *Save X amount off your next shopping order.* They look like a coupon, and they work like cash. As it is with CVS, the key to saving money at Walgreens is to only buy items that give you register rewards in return.

Here's a shopping scenario: Dove Shampoo is on sale for $4, get $4 in Register Rewards. You buy the shampoo and Walgreens gives you $4 in RRs to spend on your next purchase. You also pick up a tube of Crest Toothpaste that's on sale for $1.99, and get $1 in RRs. All told, you spend $6 out of pocket, but you walk out of the store with $5 in register rewards. Essentially, you only spent a buck on shampoo and toothpaste. Not bad, right?

If you have coupons, you could really work this deal. Say you have a MFR Dove coupon for $1.50 off and a Crest MFR coupon for $1.00 off. You'd walk out of the store with $5 in RRs, breaking even on the Crest and, making $1.50 off the Dove.

Not sure you get it?

Buy one Dove Shampoo at $4.00, get $4 in RRs

Dove Shampoo	$4.00
Dove Shampoo MFR coupon	− $1.50
TOTAL out of pocket	= $2.50
RRs returned	$4.00
TOTAL	= $1.50 Money Maker

Buy one Crest Toothpaste at $1.99, get $1 in RRs

Crest Toothpaste	$1.99
Crest MFR coupon	− $1.00
TOTAL out of pocket	$0.99
RRs returned	$1.00
TOTAL	= FREE

Like it is with CVS, the way to really work this deal is to roll your Walgreens rewards into your next purchase so you don't have to pony up any of your own cash. Plan your shopping trips so that you pay for your next purchase with your previously earned RRs. Going back to the scenario above, if you'd had register rewards from a previous trip, instead of paying $4.00 out of pocket, you'd pay in RRs and make $5.50 toward your next purchase. When a deal is a money maker, I use the store credit (RRs) to buy things like milk and eggs which I rarely have coupons for. Learn how to roll it, and you'll always have milk money!

What I love about register reward deals is that, unlike CVS, you can keep going back for more of the same awesome deal until the promotional window closes. I could work that Crest deal until my husband's sparkling grin couldn't get any sparklier!

SHOPPER'S HALL OF SHAME
Repeating Rewards

Let's go back to the Dove deal: Buy Dove Shampoo at $4.00 and get $4.00 in RRs. You cannot use previously earned Dove RRs to get another $4.00 in Dove register rewards. This is what I mean by "double dipping." You can try it, but I'm telling you right now, the register, and probably the cashier, too, won't let you do it. What you can do is use your RRs from a different deal to get more Dove Shampoo RRs. Here's how: If you had $4 in RRs from a Spend $2 on Lady Speed Stick, Get $2 in RRs, and Spend $2 on DenTek Floss, Get $2 in RRs, you could combine the rewards to buy the Dove Shampoo and get the attached $4 in RRs. What's more, you could turn right around and use those Dove RRs to buy another Lady Speed Stick and DenTek Floss and get the RRs attached to those products. You could continue to flip this deal until your bathroom cabinet overflowed.

That said, you're only allowed one of the same RR deal per transaction (register receipt), so unless you plan on "pulling a Larry" and walking in and out of the store all afternoon, you have to come back another day if you want to continue to work the same deal. Also—and this is important because so many *How to Shop for Free* newbies have learned this the hard way—you can't double dip. (See Shopper's Hall of Shame on page 92.)

One final point on Wags: In addition to register rewards, Walgreens has great in-store coupons that you can combine with MFR coupons to maximize savings. You can find them online, in the weekly circulars and in their monthly coupon book found in-store (usually up front by the circulars). *Note:* If you come across a Wags store coupon that says something like, *Limit 5*, you can use that one coupon to get all five. One coupon is all you need. Put the scissors down.

Rite Aid — Rite Aid is the latest national pharmacy chain to get into the rewards game. When you sign up for their wellness+ Rewards program, you get a card not unlike the CVS Extra Bucks card. And similarly, you need to use your card to cash in on all their weekly deals. The "wellness" card also earns you points—one point for every dollar spent. Rewards can change and vary, but typically, 125 points earns you a one-time 10 percent off shopping pass. Five hundred points scores you 10 percent off all non-prescription purchases plus a free health screening. At one thousand points, shoppers enjoy 20 percent off all nonprescription purchases every day of the week. Can you earn points by using coupons? Heck, yeah. How else would I have earned one thousand Rite Aid points?

Also, when you sign up online, you'll start receiving members-only promo deals, along with high-value coupons. And when you activate your card at www.riteaid.com, you'll receive a $5-off $25 coupon. I love those babies!

I'm coo-coo for coupons, so you better believe I registered (as should you) for a Rite Aid Video Values account online. It's gimmicky, but you can earn points for watching short videos on products you already use or want to try. For example, watch a short two-minute video on the new Schick razor and get two points toward a $5-off $20 coupon and a $1-off coupon for a new Schick razor. The movies are a bit of a snooze-fest, so I usually hit Play and walk away. I use that time to make a phone call or pour myself another cup of coffee.

At Pharmacies, Order Matters

When paying at the register, it's crucial you give the cashier your stack o' savings in the correct order to maximize the deal. If you're shopping at CVS, hand the cashier your ExtraCare card first. This will ensure you get any ECBs coming your way. Second, use your money-off coupons, like a $5-off $20 coupon. This brings down your subtotal. Then, hand over your manufacturer coupons and store coupons, and always give up your ECBs and RRs last.

Checklist
Keep it in Order 1-2-3

✓ First, hand the cashier your rewards card
✓ Next, use any money off coupons like a $5 off $20 coupon
✓ Then provide any MFR or store coupons
✓ Lastly, give the cashier your ECBs or RRs

Note: You DO NOT get cash back on ECBs or RRs. For example, if your total is $3.57 and you have RRs worth $4, you do not get the 53 cents back. You just loose the 53 cents. Sometimes, the cashier (and this seems to depend on the store you're shopping in and the cashier you're dealing with) won't even accept ECBs or RRs at a higher dollar amount than your total due. In cases like this, I just throw in something cheap, like a pack of gum or a piece of candy, to bring the price up to match the value of my reward dollars.

Miracles in the Mall

Okay, let's get out of the pharmacy and head to the mall. Many shoppers go to the mall thinking that if they find a good clearance sale, they've hit the jackpot, but what most shoppers don't realize is that they could do even better, as in FREE, if they'd do a little homework beforehand. Once I started poking around and asking questions, even I was surprised at all the deals I'd been missing. So before your next shopping trip, do yourself a favor and spend five minutes online. Chances are, your favorite store offers online coupons, added discounts, and maybe even a rewards program you didn't know about.

Checklist
Shopping the Mall for Free

- ✓ Mentally walk the mall in your mind. What are your favorite stores?
- ✓ Search your favorite store names online and add the word "coupon," "printable coupon," or "text code" after the store title (example: Ann Taylor + printable coupon) and see what pops up.
- ✓ Check www.howtoshopforfree.net for a current list of retail stores with valid coupons and sweet deals.
- ✓ Once you get to the mall, swing by the customer service desk. They usually have a printout directing you to the stores with the best deals of the day.

Some Ideas in the Beautification Department

Sephora: Free Makeover and Sultry Samples — If you can't find the makeup you simply must have for free in the pharmacies, I suggest you become a "beauty insider" at Sephora. It's free to join their rewards program, and they've got some sexy deals on makeup, skin care, and fragrances just for joining their club. The program is simple: Every time you buy, you get points. More points equal more free stuff. What's more, you'll be invited to private events and get gifted on your birthday.

The two coolest perks I discovered shopping Sephora is that when you shop online, you get three free samples for every purchase you make. Their samples change daily and there's usually about a dozen to choose from. Also, when you wander into a store, you can ask for a free sample of almost any product without purchasing a thing. Even better, you can get a ten-minute express service makeover for free. Are you thinking what I'm thinking? Stop off at Sephora before heading out Saturday night. If you're like me and you've never figured out how to get "smoky eyes," they'll whip out their brushes and show you how to flirt like a pro.

Aveda: Free Spa Services — Many of the women I know are brand-loyal when it comes to hair products, so I was thrilled to discover Aveda's Pure Privilege program because Aveda has so many loyalists. Check it out: When you become a member of Pure Privilege (there's a one-time joining fee of ten bucks), you get a free welcome gift worth thirty-some-odd-dollars in Aveda products and a birthday gift valued at twenty dollars. For every dollar you spend at an Aveda salon or retail store, you earn ten points toward amazing gifts like salon and spa services, handcrafted jewelry, and weekend getaways. Since learning how Aveda pampers its customers, I feel like I can back off and stop giving my girlfriends grief for spending money on pricey shampoo.

Victoria's Secret: Free Undies — No woman wants to get caught with her old granny panties down, so thank goodness we have Victoria's Secret to keep us stocked in new, free, and I might add—super smokin' underwear. All of my undergarments come from Victoria's Secret because I get enough coupons throughout the year to keep me covered for nothing. Here's how: Sign up for the "Angel" credit card. While it's true that I often lecture my girlfriends to stay clear of credit cards (i.e., the plastic devil), if you can promise yourself that you'll pay it off each month, carefully slip over to the dark side. You'll never have to buy panties again because they always work out for free with the coupons that Victoria's Secret sends you (and most require no additional purchase). When I first signed up for an Angel card, I got a coupon book packed with super deals, and I continue to get coupons periodically in the mail.

My favorite is the $10-off coupon. It allows me to score lotions, lip-gloss, scented candles, and sprays for nothing. My daughter loves their perfumes and scents, so I buy them at 75 percent off at the

---

HOT TIP: Pay as You Go

Anytime you charge a purchase, you can turn around and pay it off in cash. If you signed up for an Angel card to get 30 percent off your next purchase, you could charge your purchase to your Angel card to get the deal and then ask the cashier to make a payment to your card. I do this all the time. I put my purchase on the card so that I can take advantage of their discounts and promotions, and then I pay it off in cash right then and there in the store. This way, I avoid getting slapped with late charges or high interest rates. Plus, it keeps me honest. I don't buy anything I can't immediately pay for.   ✂

end-of-the-season sale and often combine them with a $10-off coupon to get them for free. I'm telling you—Victoria's Secret brings the sexy back to couponing!

Not sure you want to sign up for another credit card? No problem. If you sign up for their e-mail alerts, you become eligible for exclusive offers, and you can still cash in on their incredible semi-annual sales and in-store promotions and deals. For example, a popular "Secret Rewards" promotion encourages regular customers to buy one item for $10 to receive a secret reward worth $10, $50, $100, or $500 off your next purchase. I figured, if I buy a small bottle of perfume on sale for $10, I'll at least get my money back, making the perfume free, and if it's a good day, I'll make money off the deal. Remember—shopping for free is a numbers game. Think strategically.

Bath and Body Works: Smell Good and Don't Sweat It — Bath and Body Works doesn't have an awards card, but when you sign up for Bath and Body Works' e-mail alerts you automatically receive a free gift. Then, get ready to receive more high-value coupons and the 411 on upcoming promotions and sales. I've used Bath and Body Works' generous coupons to snag lotions, lip balm, candles, room freshener, soap, sponges, travel size items, and nail files for free. These items make perfect thank-you gifts, get-well baskets, and stocking stuffers.

The Body Shop: Girls' Night In — What could be better than enjoying a spa experience at home surrounded by your best girlfriends? When you host a Body Shop At Home party, you'll receive a complementary pampering treatment of your choice and up to $90 worth of free Body Shop products. Score! Your guests will enjoy super slashed prices on popular products, be able to indulge in spa treatments, and gain beauty tips from a Body Shop consultant. Pick from a variety of themes like Pure Pamper, indulgent bath and body party; Make

Me Fabulous, must-have make-up party; or Flawless Facial, essential skin care party.

Home Furnishings

Pottery Barn: Free Tips from the Pros — Ever wonder how to upholster furniture? Maybe you've always wanted to learn the art of floral arrangements or how to create a fabulous table display? If so, you can take classes like this at Pottery Barn for free. All you have to do is sign up. (Spots are limited and they're private events, so don't dilly-dally.) In addition to offering private classes from a pro, Pottery Barn gives you an in-store discount as a thank-you just for showing up. If you're already an interior designer who doesn't need any more masterful instruction, well then, skip the free classes and ask about Pottery Barn's designer discount.

Like it is with most retail stores, when you sign up for Pottery Barn's e-mail alerts, you'll start receiving information on exclusive sales and special promotions. And if you apply for a store credit card at Pottery Barn, for every $250 you spend, you earn $25 back. This is a deal worth considering if you're in the market for buying a big-ticket item like a sofa or media wall system. Think about it. If you charged a $2,499.00 media wall to your Pottery Barn credit card, you'd get about $250 back. Not too shabby. But remember my hard line on credit cards—pay that sucker off as you go!

Williams-Sonoma: Free Cooking Classes — If you shop at Pottery Barn, there's a good chance you frequent Williams-Sonoma, too. (They're related, you know? They belong to the same parent company.) Sign up for Williams-Sonoma email alerts and become privy to free events like culinary technique classes. Learn the art of seasoning, lessons in dairy, and how to properly sharpen a knife, for example. Each hour-long class is on the house and experts in the field of wining and dining will show you how to really impress your dinner guests.

Kohl's: Redecorate for Nothing — You can stack coupons at some retail stores by using a percent-off coupon with a dollar-off coupon, and Kohl's is my favorite place to do this. My typical combo deal at Kohl's is a $5-off coupon combined with a 15 to 30 percent-off coupon. For example, if you were buying a $10 item, Kohl's would take the $5 off first and the 30 percent off of that, making it $3.50. That's a 65% off discount of $6.50!

If you're thinking there isn't much of any value a shopper can get for ten dollars, then you haven't been to Kohl's. Using my combo deal, you'll never pay for bath towels, socks, candles, pillows, dishes, or coffee mugs again. No joke. And it's not because the store sells inferior stuff that I get so much for nothing. Au contraire, Kohl's has some of the best clearance deals out there.

Finding the best deals is a matter of looking in the right place. At Kohl's, I start my search for the deepest discounts by first looking for the Gold Star clearance racks. They're clearly marked and naturally,

---

HOT TIP: Search for Kohl's on eBay

Soon after I started shopping for free, I became an eBay junkie. One great coupon, like a Kohl's $5 off, wasn't enough. I wanted more, more, more, and eBay fed my monkey. Shopping fanatics like myself get our "addiction" satisfied by buying stacks of coupons on eBay (and yes, it's legal). This is how I always have money to play with at Kohl's. A common bid for twenty Kohl's $5-off coupons (that's a $100 value) is under two bucks. *Doesn't that sound too good to be true?* In Chapter 6: The Business of Buying, I'll give you the scoop on how to find and buy the coupons you want and need from the best sellers on eBay.   ✂

I hit the 80 percent off rack first. My goal is always to find something that's marked down to approximately five bucks because then I can use a $5-off coupon to make it nearly free.

You Asked It

Q: *How do get your hands on those awesome $5-off coupons?*

A: *Sign up online to receive Kohl's e-mail alerts, and they will send you a $5-off coupon. If you sign up for a Kohl's credit card (here I go again pushing plastic), you'll receive a discount for 10 percent off your first purchase. Some select Kohl's will even offer a $10-off coupon for signing up in the store (I feel another coupon high coming on). Once you become a Kohl's card holder you can save 15, 20, and 30 percent off your entire purchase on select days. Plus, they offer scratch cards to card holders—kind of like Lottery tickets—at the register where you can scratch away more savings. I swear, it's like they don't want you to spend any money in the store, and that's why I love Kohl's.*

Home Improvement Centers

Home Depot: Major Discounts on Big Projects — When you sign up for Home Depot's Home Improver Club online, you will be alerted of free workshops and classes in your area. My favorite is the Do-It-Herself series. These are classes geared toward wannabe tough chicks who want to learn more about handling power tools and outsmarting our men around the house. When you take one of Home Depot's classes, you learn something new, and they often reward you with a high-value coupon to redeem in the store. *I am woman. Hear me score!*

Another freebie I discovered at Home Depot is the "contractor's bid." Shhhh, you do not have to provide proof that you're a contractor to take advantage of this deal. How it works: If you're planning to do

---

SHOPPER'S
Hall of Fame

"I've found deep discounts on new appliances by shopping the back of the store. Sure, some of them have a ding here and a scratch there, but if it's on the back of a stove or a fridge, no one's ever going to see it, right? Also, look for great package deals, like—buy a fridge and a stove—get the dishwasher for free. That's what I did, although looking back, I wish I'd done a little consumer research beforehand. My refrigerator shelves buckled when I loaded them with twenty half gallons of free iced tea. Next time, I'm in the market for a big appliance, I'm going to check out www.Overstock.com. They have reduced prices on appliances and offer $2.95 shipping on any order—refrigerators included!"

Kim, Newburyport, Massachusetts

---

a sizable renovation or home improvement project, figure out what the raw materials (i.e., lumber, tile, steel) will end up costing you. If you're fairly certain you'll spend over $2,500 to complete the job, you can request a contractor's bid. *Note:* Go to the contractor's service counter, not a regular register. You will more than likely see a sign that explains that if you buy $2,500 in material, you can request a bid. A Home Depot manager will review your plans and estimated costs and get back to you within 24 hours with a bid. Usually their costs are 10 to 15 percent lower than what you originally planned on spending. Plus, if you have coupons, you can stack additional savings on top of their offer. (A lot of contractors use coupons, so don't be afraid to use them.) I saved $1,700 on my outside decking this way. Also, should you be doing interior work to your house, consider switching to eco-friendly appliances. You can often get a sizable tax credit for doing so, and Home Depot offers old appliance haul-away for free.

Lowe's: Free Classes for Kids — Where Home Depot offers the Do-It-Herself workshops that I love, Lowe's has their Build and Grow clinics for kids. Just take your kid into any Lowe's on a Saturday at 10:00 a.m. to build a free wooden project, like a baseball game during spring training or a garden planter for Earth Day. Also, each child gets a free apron, a set of goggles, and a certification of completion. How cool is that?

Another awesome customer service at Lowe's is the 10% off veteran discount. Just ask for your money-off discount at checkout and be prepared to show proof of service. Your DD-214 (the official document issued upon retirement, separation, or discharge from active-duty military), along with your driver's license is usually all the proof you need.

Also, Lowe's and Home Depot tend to have similar markdowns, and they accept each other's coupons, so it's worth scoping out both stores for the best savings opportunity. If you've recently moved, keep your eyes out for a welcome packet from the post office full of highly desired coupons, including super savings from Home Depot and Lowe's. Do not throw this moving packet away with the bubble wrap!

HOT TIP: Match Prices

Both Home Depot and Lowe's do price matching. If you find a lower price on an item at Lowe's, Home Depot will match that price and beat it by 10 percent. All you have to do is bring in the competing store ad with the listed sale price. A lot of stores do price matching, so remember to do your homework before you shop! You may be spending money you could be keeping in your wallet.   ✄

Office Supplies

Staples: Let the Ink Run Out — Sign up for Staples Rewards and when you take your old printer cartridges to Staples, they'll give you two bucks back in Staples play money to spend on anything in the store, including a new cartridge. Plus, you get 10% back on all ink and toner purchases. You can recycle up to ten cartridges a month per customer when you present your rewards card, so sign up for the free card. *Note:* All cartridges are accepted for recycling, but to be sure they qualify for Ink Recycling Rewards, check with your local store or online for details. If you're a *How to Shop for Free* "printer" versus a "clipper," this is totally the way to go because, as you know, ink is expensive and it runs out fast, so saving a couple bucks here and there is a good thing. Ten cartridges a month is a $20 value and you can stack coupons on top of Staples rewards to increase your free spending budget. If I don't roll my savings right back into more ink, I fill up my cart with office supplies that always work out for free, like power cords, pens, markers, Sharpies, and paper.

OfficeMax: Save Some Green — The MaxPerks free program works similarly to the one at CVS. Swipe your MaxPerks rewards card at checkout (online or in-store) and get money taken off your total bill when you buy specified items. Rewards dollars can be used on any future deals, so be sure to use your card every time you make a purchase. The best MaxPerks give you 100% back in Bonus Rewards, making your purchase totally free. Pick up the weekly ad in-store or peruse their killer deals online and cash in.

As for going "green," OfficeMax has gotten into the spirit, offering MaxPerks members $3 in rewards for each qualifying ink or toner cartridge dropped off in an OfficeMax store location. Members are welcome to recycle up to 20 cartridges a month. That's $60 in rewards dollars!

Pet Stores

PetSmart: Free Pet Food and Treats — The best way I've found to get pet food, toys, trinkets, and snacks for little to nothing is by signing up for "Pet Perks." Enrollment is free and when you sign up online (surely you're noticing the perks of online membership by now), PetSmart will send you a welcome kit worth up to $250 in coupons redeemable in any PetSmart stores. With this loaded welcome wagon, why wouldn't you jump on board? You'll also receive e-mail notification of bottom-dollar deals and discounts in the store that regular customers can't get. That's right—members only, baby. And if that's not enough, your pet will be gifted on his or her birthday.

As you well know by now, you can combine MFR coupons with in-store deals to stretch savings. I cashed in on a PetSmart offer that gave me a free collar when I bought a bag of Nature's Best brand dog food. I had MFR coupons for Nature's Best, making the dog food and the collar free. Hot diggidy-dog! Keep your eye out for deals like this. I've been able to score free dog food for years by combining in-store deals with manufacturer coupons.

PETCO: Free Kibble and Pet Shampoo — PETCO PALS is free to join, and once you do, you become eligible to cash in on exclusive in-store deals. Rumor has it that PETCO has 200 to 300 different products specially discounted in-store for PALS members on any given day. Check the weekly store circular for the biggest steals. And go online to find high-value coupons and coupon codes for further savings.

Also, PALS members are invited to participate in two purchase rewards programs: The Buy 10, Get 1 Bag Free and The Buy 8, Get 1 Free Grooming Service. After you've purchased ten bags of the same brand and size premium dry dog or cat food within a twelve-month period, PETCO will send you a coupon for a free bag. Similarly, after eight Full-Service Grooms or eight Baths within twelve months, PETCO will mail you a Free Groom or Free Bath coupon.

HOT TIP: Check the Bag and Ask the Vet

Check every bag of pet food for high-value coupons. Sometimes, and especially with new products, you'll find a coupon in the bag that'll essentially get you another bag for free. When I unearth this kind of savings, I can't help rolling the deal. I'll go back for another bag containing another free coupon, use that coupon to get another bag, and so on and so on.

If digging around in a sixteen pound bag of dog food isn't your thing, then try asking your vet for coupons. Vets get fantastic high-value coupons that they're more than happy to hand over to you and your furry pal.   ✄

Bookstores

Borders: Perks on Name Brand Products — The Borders Rewards Program is free and you earn "Borders Bucks" every time you make a purchase in-store or at Borders.com, plus members receive weekly coupons and exclusive in-store offers via e-mail. In my opinion, the coolest thing Borders offers is their "Perks" program, where members get hooked up with savings on their favorite brands and retailers like Smashbox Cosmetics, Bloomingdale's, and Kate Spade. You can even join a wine club through Borders and be first in line to cash in on top travel deals. Who knew?

Barnes and Noble: Bonus Coupons — Unlike Borders, membership with B & N isn't free, but the $25 fee quickly pays for itself after a purchase or two. Hardcover best sellers are always 40 percent off, and you can often throw additional promo codes on top of that to make the deal even sweeter. Plus, as soon as you sign up you get loaded with bonus coupons and are tipped off to exclusive deals. You can also use your member card to get discounts on panini sandwiches and coffee drinks at the café.

Independent Bookstores: Unique Perks — Depending on where you live, your local independent bookstore is likely to have its own unique rewards program for loyal customers. Ask your local bookseller what specific benefits (free stuff) it offers the next time you're shopping for the latest IndieBound release.

Amazon: Cash Back — Amazon.com automatically sends you thirty bucks after your first purchase with the Amazon Rewards Visa card. I realize we've been talking about books, but let me remind you that Amazon sells more than books, so don't be afraid to shop in other categories. There are many interesting deals lurking around that site.

My first Amazon.com order was for king size sheets. I found four sets of sheets that, with shipping, totaled twenty-four bucks. They could have been *used* and this still would have been an unbelievable deal! I signed up for the credit card, placed my order, and within days received my sheets and my first bill with a $30 cash credit. Since the sheets were only $24, I made six bucks on the deal. And if that wasn't already awesome, I earned three rewards points for every dollar I spent. Cha-ching. Thank you, Amazon.com.

Stationery

Hallmark: Free Birthday Gifts — Hallmark's known to offer printable $5-off coupons for its Gold Crown rewards members. There's always something for five dollars or less at Hallmark, and these little gifts come in handy for birthdays and holidays. I have a stockpile of cards on hand, which means I never miss anyone's birthday or big day.

Before we move on to the next section, I want to make the point that the list of mall and online stores above is not all-inclusive. If it were, this would be a much, much longer chapter, and we need to move on; we've got a lot of ground to cover. Simply know that there are great deals to be had if only you go looking, so be sure to seek them out. Chances are your favorite stores have rewards programs that offer fabulous freebies, coupons, and perks.

Other Ways to Get Something for Nothing

There are numerous ways to save once you start asking questions and looking around. So, always ask. Push a little. Until you find out otherwise, assume that you can get a better deal than the one you have now. What I've discovered is that pretty much everything you spend your hard-earned money on can be negotiated. It's just that most of us dutifully fork over top dollar prices without even questioning whether or not we can get a better deal. I hope to encourage you to start asking questions because there are many ways to enjoy life for less. That said, sometimes in order to get the unexpected deals, you have to put on the mean girl face. In other words, you have to be willing to play hardball.

Phone, Internet, and Cable

It doesn't make sense to me that as a valued customer who pays her bills on time every month, I can't simply ask for my rates to be renegotiated in return for my good behavior. I've tried this approach, and it's never gotten me very far. So I now use the threat of cancellation to get what I want. I admit, I feel a little like Carmela Soprano acting out this way, but on the other hand, it does seem to work. I can't promise you that it'll work every time, but should you want to give it a try, I recommend you practice this command: *Give me what I want or I'll find someone who will.*

I've had success getting my monthly cable and phone bills down by calling up my providers and asking them to renegotiate with me for a better package. If they tell me they can't help me out, I tell them I'm prepared to take my business somewhere else. Because most companies fear the word "cancellation" more than any other, they almost always find a way to keep me happy. Rather suddenly, they offer me a better plan. Just like that.

If the tough-chick act doesn't work, you have other options. Try looking into phone services like Vonage, www.vonage.com, or Skype, www.skype.com, for unlimited local, long distance, and international calls on the cheap. See if your company or employer offers discounts on phone service. Until I just had to have a Droid, I used prepaid cell phone service and a pay-as-you-go plan to control over-usage and costs. I highly recommend it, especially if you're paying the bill for gabby teenagers in the house. I know many people who have bundled their phone, cable, and Internet together for reduced savings. Finally, if you're on a limited budget, you might qualify for a reduced rate from the phone company and even a free phone. Visit www.safelink.com to see if you do.

Gym Membership

If your gym is hiking up their annual rate or monthly fees, shop around and see what the competitors are offering. If you find another gym with better benefits, see if your current gym will match that price. Mine did. You can also check with your health insurance company. Most people don't realize they can get reimbursed for working out. (This makes squeezing into those compression shorts a little more comfortable, yes?) Our insurance company reimburses us $100 per person per year, which leaves me with little to no excuse for avoiding the gym.

Movie Rentals

Surely, you've heard about Redbox by now. Redbox kiosks seem to be popping up every time you blink. Go online, www.redbox.com, to find the closest Redbox location near you. Redbox DVD rentals are only a buck a day, but when you sign up for a redbox.com account, you'll receive a free movie code by e-mail. These monthly codes can also be found online at code-swapping sites (totally legit, by the way) by doing a simple search for "Redbox + code." Once you have a code, enter it onscreen at a Redbox kiosk, swipe your credit card, and you'll receive a one-day free rental. The more codes you find, the more free movies you can get. (You have to watch them within 24 hours though, or they won't be free!)

Another great way to score movies (and support your community) is to visit your local library. If you haven't been in a while, you may be surprised by their impressive and current selection of DVDs, CDs, and books on tape. The library also often has free and discounted passes to local museums, aquariums, and amusement parks.

Gasoline

Filling up your gas tank for free is a challenge, but I've managed to pull it off, and with a little dedication, so can you. First of all, find out if your grocery store or warehouse club offers gas points. How most gas promotions work is that you earn a certain number of gas points per dollar spent, so the more you spend the more you can save per gallon. If your store offers a gas deal, it's available to every shopper with a reward/loyalty card. Typically, your points from several shopping trips can be combined and used together for one fat fill-up, but be sure to find out *if* they have to be redeemed within a specific time frame and what gas stations are participating in the promotion.

How I work it: I get the highest number of gas points by asking the cashier to hit the subtotal button *before* I hand over my rewards card and coupons. Hitting the subtotal button triggers the cash register to calculate the number of gas points awarded to a customer, so to get the highest number of points, I ask the cashier to hit subtotal before my savings are factored in. Since my average grocery bill is $200 to $300 before I whittle it down to nothing, I'm able to rack up gas points quickly. My personal best was the day I paid nine cents a gallon after accumulated points. I can certainly justify driving up and down the North Shore searching for bargains for *that* price.

WORK IT: GET YOUR REWARD

Before we move on to Chapter 6: The Business of Buying, I want you to sign up for at least one rewards program. Just one. If I have my way, you'll sign up for the CVS Extra Care program because it's so quick and easy to start realizing the benefits, but do what you want. Just do something. And thank me later.   ✄

HOT TIP: Practice Old-Fashioned Bartering

There's nothing better than the old-fashioned barter system. Since teaching myself how to shop for free, I've been approached by many people who have offered up their professional services in exchange for what I know and am sharing with you now. This is how I "pay" to keep my house cleaned and my hair cut and styled. I even bartered with our construction guy to get my laundry room built in exchange for coupon tips. (It was his idea, by the way.) I love doing business using the barter system, and I bet if you think about it for five minutes, you'd realize that you, too, have a specialty and knowledge to barter.   ✄

Resources

Amazon: www.Amazon.com

Aveda: www.Aveda.com

Barnes and Noble: www.BarnesandNoble.com

Bath and Body Works: www.BathandBodyWorks.com

The Body Shop: www.thebodyshopathome.com

Borders: www.Borders.com

CVS: www.cvs.com

Hallmark: www.Hallmark.com

Home Depot: www.HomeDepot.com

Kohl's: www. Kohls.com

Lowe's: www.lowes.com

OfficeMax: www.officemax.com

Petco: www.petco.com

PetSmart: www.PetSmart.com

Pottery Barn: www.potterybarn.com

Redbox: www.redbox.com/

Rite Aid: www.riteaid.com/wellness

Sephora: www.Sephora.com

Skype: www.skype.com

Staples: www.Staples.com

Victoria's Secret: www.VictoriasSecret.com

Vonage: www.vonage.com/

Walgreens: www.walgreens.com

6

The Business of Buying

If you've gotten this far into the book, I think it's safe to say you have some serious hard-core shopper in you, so I hope it thrills you to know that we're just getting started. Next, we'll explore a practice popular in the couponing subculture: buying coupons. *Buying coupons?* Isn't that, like, cheating? I don't think so, but you be the judge.

What's in the cart?

Here's what you'll find in this chapter:

- The advantages of buying coupons on eBay
- The difference between clipping services and online sellers
- How trading groups work
- How to get fantastic freebies just for talking up new products.

What Idiot Would Pay for a Coupon?

My husband used to buy a Mickey D's coffee every day on his way to work. He said to me, "Babe, I want to *at least* buy my own coffee."

I'm sorry, but to whom does he think he's married? I just couldn't have him spending money on coffee every day when I could go to eBay (which I did) and spend $5 for 100 coupons for free McDonald's coffee. I proceeded to take the money out of his wallet and line it with coffee coupons. I said, "No problem, honey. Buy your own coffee." Poor guy—he doesn't even get to splurge with me around.

I've gotten into debates with more conventional shoppers (i.e., those unimaginative types who think they have to pay full retail price) who don't understand my love affair with coupons. The more adamant dissenters have tried to convince me, "But Kathy, coupons have no value." Well, then. Do a quick search for coupons on eBay and then tell me coupons aren't worth anything. Right now, hundreds of thousands of coupons are being bought and sold on eBay. Yes, those little squares of paper that you pay nothing for demand a competitive price on the world's largest online auction and shopping website. Still, what kind of idiot would pay for coupons? The kind who knows a genius money-saving strategy when she sees one. Listen up, shoppers: You can buy multiples of almost any high-value coupon on eBay for dirt-cheap and save yourself valuable time.

Let's say your local grocery store is having a deal where your favorite Crystal Light Drink Mix is on sale for $1, and a coupon for *$2-off two Crystal Light On The Go Drink Mix* appears in the Sunday inserts. (By now you know that with this winning combination, you could stock up on free iced tea for the entire summer. Talk about your sweet tea.) But instead of spending your limited time collecting multiple inserts, cutting and/or printing coupons, you simply buy multiples of this one coupon on eBay from someone who already did all the work for you. Plus, it'll hardly cost you anything. The last time I looked, the average bid for twenty *$2-off two Crystal Light On The Go Drink Mix* coupons was $0.99. Can I get a— Woo Hoo Deal Alert!

You Asked It

Q: Isn't it illegal to sell coupons?

A: Per eBay's rules and those written on most coupons that state, "Void if transferred, sold, auctioned to any person," it is illegal to sell coupons. The way a seller gets around this (and this is totally legal, BTW) is to charge buyers for the time and energy it takes the seller to locate, collect, cut, package, and advertise their coupons. In actuality, when you "buy" coupons on eBay, you're paying for a service, not the coupons themselves. Most sellers will make note of this by including language on the auction page like, "In accordance with eBay policy, these coupons are FREE. You are paying for the time it took for me to acquire, list, and send these coupons to you."

The More the Mightier

Not only can you buy multiples of individual coupons on eBay and have them sent directly to your doorstep or inbox, you can bid on entire inserts. If you're someone who doesn't want to mess around with buying multiples of the Sunday paper or dig them out of recycling bins, this could be the perfect solution for you. The starting bid on five uncut SmartSource, RedPlum, General Mills, or P&G inserts is usually 99 cents. That's a whole lot cheaper than buying five Sunday papers—even if you get them from the dollar store. That's not to say that the final bid won't be higher (but probably only by a few bucks), but that's the game you play with eBay. The only real downside I see to bidding on inserts, and it's a minor one, is that by the time the auction closes and you receive your inserts in the mail, you're a week behind. Most often, this is no biggie because weekly store sales don't always coincide with the coupons issued that week. (Usually I'm working deals with coupons that were issued the previous month.) Just beware that if you're hoping to combine coupons from the inserts you're bidding on with a current store deal that has a short five-to-seven-day promotional window, you may be out of luck.

An alternative to bidding on eBay and waiting for an auction to close is to choose the *Buy It Now* button. This locks your purchase in at a set price. When you "Buy It Now," the item is yours. This saves you from starting all over if you've been outbid in an auction. Warning: Make sure you check the shipping cost before you hit the *Buy It Now* button.

My son is famous for screaming "Oh My Gosh, a Webkinz (last year's must-have toy) is only 99 cents, but I have to buy it in thirty seconds! Mom, can I buy it? Can I buy it?"

"What are the shipping costs," I calmly ask.

"Um . . . eighteen dollars and ninety-nine cents."

"That's not a good deal. You can go down the street and buy it for less."

His father's no better. He falls for the big WHOOPS every time. I'll never forget the time he went nuts over a log splitter he found for dirt cheap in Pennsylvania. I said, "Honey, look at the shipping costs. It says local pickup only. That's *three* states away." Luckily another fool outbid him.

Checklist

Buying on eBay

- ✓ **Use the Search Button.** Search for the specific name of the coupon you want using "product + coupon."
- ✓ **Don't Forget to Read the Fine Print.** How many coupons are you bidding on? What's the value of the coupon— $0.50 off/1 or $0.50 off/2? These little details make a big difference. And check the expiration dates. If they expire before you get them, you've wasted your money.
- ✓ **Buy It Now.** This is the fastest and easiest way to place an order. Just remember to read the shipping costs before you hit *Buy It Now*.

Because I'm religious about getting multiple Sunday inserts I don't buy a ton of coupons on eBay (you know me, I don't like to spend a dime if I don't have to), but I purchase a fair share. For example, I often buy coupons for my daughter's favorite Japanese Yakisoba noodle soup on eBay. I buy sixty $0.50-off coupons at a time and have them sent directly to her. The coupons double to a dollar off in her college town making the soup free, so if she turns up her nose at the cafeteria food, I know she won't starve.

WORK IT: SEARCH "FAVORITE PRODUCT + COUPON"

Search eBay for savings on products you always need or for stores you frequently patronize. Go ahead—be very YOU specific. When it comes to coffee, my husband's a McDonald's loyalist. You, on the other hand, might refuse to drink anything other than coffee from Starbuck's or Coffee Bean. What's your personal taste? Search exactly for what you want. I think you'll be amazed at what you can get your hands on for a nominal fee.   ✂

You Asked It

Q: If several people are selling the same coupons, how do you know whose best to buy from?

A: The first thing you want to look for is the top-rated seller badge to the right of the item up for auction. This is a strong indicator that you can trust the seller. Once you've found a top-rated seller with the goods you're looking for, follow the link to the seller's page. Again, look to the right of the product description. You'll notice a number in parenthesis next to the seller's eBay user name. That number corresponds to the number of transactions the seller has had, so the higher the number, the more seasoned the seller. Underneath that number, you'll notice a percentage. This corresponds to buyer feedback. Obviously, 100 percent positive buyer feedback is the best you can hope for.

This percentage is based on how accurate the product descriptions are and how quickly items ship. If previous customers were happy, chances are you'll be, too. As a general rule, I buy from sellers with a 98 to 100 percent feedback rate. On the off chance you do get scammed and you don't receive your items, or if something shows up on your doorstep that doesn't at all match what you paid for, eBay will take care of it. All your purchases are covered by eBay Buyer Protection.

Fantastic Finds

Okay, now that you know how to score grocery coupons on eBay, let me explain how to get discounts on the gorgeous girly stuff, like

---

HOT TIP: Search Across State Lines

A word of warning: This is an advanced shopping strategy designed for the truly obsessed. When you cross state lines, you can often score better coupons. Here's why: Coupon values often differ state to state as they do among papers around the country. While the Sunday SmartSource (SS) insert in Massachusetts will look almost identical to the SS insert in Arizona, the coupon values within the inserts may vary. For example, the Massachusetts insert may contain a coupon for $1 off/2 tubes of Colgate Kids toothpaste, while the Arizona insert may have a $0.50-off/1 coupon for the same product. In this scenario, the coupon issued in Arizona is the one I want because when doubled, it's $1 off/1 tube and I can often find Colgate Kids toothpaste on sale in my hood for a buck. If I'm running low on toothpaste for the kids, it might be worth my while to buy a stack of $0.50-off coupons from another state on eBay. (An Arizona issued MFR coupon is good in any

---

clothes, pampering services, and household jewels. For starters, go back to Chapter 5: Like Getting Paid to Shop and choose a retail outlet you want to find discount coupons for. Once you start searching on eBay, you'll quickly discover ridiculous savings for nearly any store you can think of. I mentioned before that I'm a Kohl's die-hard shopper. The number one reason I go crazy in that store is because I'm usually armed with twenty Kohl's $5-off coupons that I scored on eBay for 99 cents. Shoppers, that's $99.00 of totally free stuff. I'd be a fool *not* to go a little wild.

Wherever you like to shop, do an eBay search for the "store name + coupon" and see what kind of red-hot deals could be yours just for

---

state.) To find out if another state has a better deal, I simply do a search on eBay for the coupon value I want. Don't search coupons by state. That'll get you nowhere. Simply search for the coupon value you *hope* exists. I've been playing the coupon game long enough to know that if I find a $1-off/2 coupon in my Massachusetts inserts, there's bound to be another for $0.50 off/1 out there somewhere. Using the example above, I'd search "Colgate toothpaste + .50 coupon" on eBay to see if this, or a similar deal, existed. Or better yet, I'd just search "Colgate + coupon," and all the coupons for Colgate will pop up. If a $0.50 off/1 coupon exists, I'm likely to find confirmation of the value I'm looking for. Again, manufacturer coupons are good in all states so you don't need to worry about liability. If in doubt, ask the seller to send you an enlarged photocopy of the fine print as it appears on the coupon before you *Buy It Now.*   ✂

placing a small bid. If your search doesn't produce any results, try searching the "store name + gift card." Just as it is with coupons, thousands of unused gift cards are being bought, sold, and swapped daily on eBay and other gift card exchange sites like, www.plasticjungle.com and www.cardpool.com. Generally, gift cards are pricier than coupons because their dollar value is so much higher, but you can usually knock 25 percent off the total value of the card. For example, a $200 J Crew gift card might sell for $160 on eBay. Not free, but if you know you're going to be dropping change in J Crew anyway, buying a discounted gift card on eBay beforehand will save you some bucks at the register.

HOT TIP: Don't Forget the Code

There's always more to be had and money to be saved if you take the time to look. When you're shopping online, always do a search for a promo or coupon code before you pay for the items in your cart. Almost always, you can get your total cost down if you do a little homework beforehand. Generally search the Web or within the online store you're shopping for a promo code. If you come up empty try sites like www .retailmenot.com or www.couponseven.com where thousands of online promo codes for a wide variety of retailers are free. If you still don't find what you're looking for, go back to eBay. Just like coupons and gift cards, promo codes are bought and sold daily on eBay. It might seem ridiculous to pay for an on-line code, but spending a buck or two for a code that will give you 20 percent off your total sale is actually a really great deal. Think about it: If you're spending $100, 20 percent off your total sale would give you twenty bucks back. Do the math! Isn't spending two bucks worth saving twenty?   ✄

Moonlighting

If bidding on coupons isn't your thing, no problem. You have options:
individual sellers and clipping services.

Individual Sellers

Often, individual sellers who got their start selling on eBay eventually
move their goods to an independent site where they can escape
eBay's fees and maintain control over their business. Other sellers will
keep their eBay store and additionally operate an independent site.
Periodically, I receive messages from my top eBay sellers offering
coupons through their independent shops, promising lower prices,
instant delivery, and no registration cost.

If you find sellers you like and trust on eBay, send them a message
and ask if they operate an indie site. Sellers on eBay are prohibited
from advertising any personal sites they have on their eBay sellers'
pages. Once they sell to you, however, you become *their* customer, and
they can make contact with you outside of eBay, or vice versa—you to
them. I've found that the coupon sellers who run their own sites are

often trying to make a living doing so and therefore, take their business seriously. They know that if they jerk people around, they'll quickly be shut down. Because you're not covered like you are on eBay, buying from an independent seller is a risk, but often the investment is so small (it's not like you're buying gem stones), it can be a risk worth taking. I won't invest more than 99 cents on an independent site until I'm satisfied that they're not conning me. If dependable, I'll bump up my order the next time around and I pay for my order via PayPal, so my purchases are protected.

Clipping Services

An online clipping service is usually staffed by several devoted (i.e., like me) shoppers who diligently collect, clip, organize, package, and ship millions of coupons to those of us who want to take life easy while others do all the work. I totally support this business plan and love that one can order bundles of coupons from a clipping service for pennies. Remember: You're paying the handling fee, not for the coupons themselves. Search the web for "coupon clipping service," and you'll find several to choose from.

HOT TIP: Don't Pay for Printables

Steer clear of buying Internet printables from an independent seller and only order actual coupons clipped from the Sunday inserts or other paper sources. Unfortunately, you have little to no way of knowing if the printable coupon being advertised online is the real deal or a photocopy of a fake. Plus, why pay for printables that you, your friends, or family, can print at home?   ✄

> **HOT TIP:** Get a Sneak Peak
>
> You can also get a sneak peek of the Sunday inserts by visiting www.sundaycouponpreview.com/ where the weekly contents of RedPlum and SmartSource are posted the Friday before.   ✂

When I want to score multiples of a coupon that correspond to an awesome upcoming sale, and I can't find them on eBay, or I don't want to run the risk of being outbid on eBay, I'll scan online clipping services. (*Note:* Some coupon services limit how many of one coupon you can buy so there's enough to go around for everyone. On eBay, I can go *girl gone wild* and buy as many as I want.)

You Asked It

Q: *How do I find out ahead of time what next week's sales will be?*

A: *This is the short answer: It depends on the store. Ask your local grocery, drug, and home improvement stores if they release their upcoming sale flyers ahead of time. One of my favorite grocers will give me the ad on Monday for the sale that starts on Friday. (I have to make a point of asking for it.) On the flip side, I've had cashiers at other stores scrutinize me, like I've asked for contraband secrets. In these situations, I want to say, "You work in retail, not for the CIA. Now give me my damn ad!"*

Both CVS and Walgreen's publish a preview every Thursday of their upcoming sale starting on Sunday. Rite Aid will often release their upcoming ad and rebate deals if you ask a cashier in the store. Kmart posts their upcoming ad on their site, www.kmart.com. If I spot a killer deal in any of these stores, I get a jump on ordering multiples from eBay, an independent seller, or a clipping service because, come Sunday, those hot sale items will go fast. Plus, if I place a coupon order on Thursday, I'm likely to have them in hand by Sunday or Monday.

Another added benefit to using a clipping service is that you can pre-order coupons for products you normally buy every week. For example, my kids go meow for tuna fish sandwiches. I'll order sixty Bumble Bee tuna coupons at one time and when a local grocery store puts Bumble Bee on sale, I pounce on the deal and stockpile. A word of warning: If you pre-order coupons, make sure what you're purchasing won't expire for at least a month. You wouldn't want to be stuck with hundreds of coupons that had to be redeemed in a matter of days.

Trading Groups

I told you to never throw away coupons because you never know when you might decide to use them and also because coupons are like cash in your wallet—a form of currency that can be used as leverage. Think about it—wouldn't it be cool to exchange your unwanted coupons for the savings you really desire? That's what trading groups are for. And if you ask me, trading coupons should be the new stock market. At least if you crash your cart, you don't go bankrupt.

Do an online search for "coupon trading group" or "coupon trading sites" and you'll discover hundreds of trading sites where women are swapping coupons from baby bum powder to hair color. Just about every coupon site, including www.howtoshopforfree.net, has an online trading forum. On my site, users post their "wish list"—the coupons they want—along with what they're willing to give up in exchange.

You will find sites out there that are set up exclusively for coupon trading, and most of these are free to join. If you're not into trading

"I will often purchase multiple papers when there are good coupons, but that can get awfully expensive at four bucks each. So when the really GREAT coupons come out, and I could use a few extras, I turn to clipping services. Recently, I ordered twenty $3-off any bag of Purina One cat food coupons from a clipping service for six dollars. Several stores had the small 3.5-pound bags on clearance for under $3.00, so I used my twenty coupons to score over sixty pounds of cat food free. The only money I spent OOP was the six bucks I paid the clipping service for the coupons."

Christine, Groton, Massachusetts

online and prefer shopper-to-shopper interaction, you might try searching for a trading group on www.meetup.com. Through Meetup, hundreds of groups all over the country get together on a monthly basis to talk shop and swap savings. I started my own group of like-minded coupon freaks who come over to my house, and, while our kids run wild, we drink wine, gossip, and trade our stash. *Note:* The deal with trading groups is that your coupons work as cash, so additional money is never exchanged. In fact, it's a no-no to ask for a fee when trading.

Spread the Word

You can get amazing, exclusive high-value deals just for trying out new products and spreading the word. Am I talking about product testing? You bet I am. Does this make you cringe? If you just nodded your head, I'm going to guess that either you don't like the idea of being "bought off" for your positive feedback and/or you don't want your shopping choices to be tracked because it feels like an invasion of privacy. Well, unless you've never signed up for a store loyalty card, Club card, or even used the Internet, some amount of information about your shopping habits has already been tracked. *Don't freak.* Before you let Big Brother paranoia take over, try to think of it this way: Retailers are just using the information they gather about you to give you more of what you want. To that, I say, "Thank you very much." If Procter & Gamble wants to spend their time and energy crafting a special marketing message that speaks directly to me—go for it. I'll listen. I've found that the more info and feedback I provide a store or manufacturer about my likes and dislikes, the more tailor-made freebies that come flying through my door.

HOT TIP: Look Paranoia in the Face

You can always investigate a store's privacy policy to better understand how they're using your personal info. If they're selling your personal details to other outside parties, they're legally required to come clean and state their intentions clearly. For example, at www.pg.com, one can find a link to their Privacy Notice at the bottom of their homepage. P&G's privacy notice states that "We use the information we collect to provide the products and services you request, to tell you about other products and services offered by P&G, and to manage our sites and services. . . . In general, we do not share your personal information with third-party marketers, unless we have asked for and obtained your explicit consent."   ✄

Here are some key sites/groups that offer great savings in exchange for a shout out:

Vocalpoint — Vocalpoint is a Procter & Gamble program that promotes itself as a "community of women that provides valuable and interesting insights about new products, surveys, daily tips, articles, and coupons/samples." Translation: product testing. Once you've signed up with Vocalpoint, you'll become eligible for high-value coupons. If you want to get the best deals, the trick is to stay involved. The more you log onto the site and participate in their polls, focus groups, and surveys, the more you'll be rewarded. One of the coolest things about Vocalpoint is that they send their members multiples of high-value coupons. (They want you to share with others. Of course that doesn't mean you *have* to. Well, at least not every time.) The first package I got from Vocalpoint included a small sample box of a new P & G cereal, along with a coupon to try a full-size box for free and several $1.50-off/1 box coupons. I got all this just for giving my opinion. *There's more of that where that came from!*

BzzAgent — BzzAgent touts itself as the leading word-of-mouth media and marketing company with a community of 650,000 people who help influence some of the biggest companies in the world. BzzAgent is free to join and when you become an "agent," you get to sample free products in exchange for your feedback. In other words, the door is open for big mouths. Like it is with Vocalpoint, BzzAgent wants you to share your opinion ("Have you tried the latest Old El Paso jalapeño dip? It's the schiznit," said one woman to another at the gym.), but where Vocalpoint is centered on the P & G brand, BzzAgent introduces its users to a variety of brands and encourages you to be outspoken and promote your favorites.

Pssst — Pssst is a General Mills site that taps its members for input on their newest product launches. Membership is free, and, as a thank-you for your honest opinions, you'll receive GM samples and coupons.

Kraft First Taste — If you're crazy for Kraft, here's your chance to try new Kraft products before anyone else does. Join the Kraft community and get the inside scoop on the latest Kraft creations, receive free samples, and weigh in on your likes and dislikes for further discounts.

ALL YOU Reality Checker — *ALL YOU* magazine is available exclusively on Walmart newsstands and when you become an *ALL YOU* Reality Checker at www.allyou.com, you join Walmart's community of savvy shoppers. Participate in surveys, swap savings tips, and test new products, and if your voice stands above the rest, you could be chosen to appear in *ALL YOU*.

House Party — House Parties are by far the coolest product-tasting gimmick I've come across. Basically, if you're chosen to participate in this exclusive club, you get to party down with your friends and family courtesy of a wide variety of participating sponsors like Williams-Sonoma, Hasbro, Nestlé, and Shutterfly.

When you host a House Party, you and your peeps are first in line to try new products in your own home and walk away with crazy coupons, new recipes, and goodie bags. Plus, based on who you are and what you're into, you choose to host the parties that best suit you. Into French food and wine? Mais oui! Put on your best party dress for continental cocktail hour. Like to get your game on? Ask your colleagues to join you for Hasbro game night. Having a baby? Invite the girls over for a Gerber baby shower. Like to look good without starving to death? Host the Fun, Fit, and Fab party where guests work out and cool down with fat-free chocolate mousse.

While I swear by these tricks of the trade, there's one more important thing here: I want to give you permission to take it or leave it. Buying coupons on eBay might be something you want to try, while hosting a French cocktail party isn't your style. While it's true that there are endless deals to be had, that doesn't mean you have to jump on all of them. Pick and choose. I'm simply giving you options and then you decide what you want to try. Play around. See what works for you.

WORK IT: TAKE IT OR LEAVE IT

Whether it's bidding on a gift card from www.plasticjungle.com, joining a coupon-trading group, or signing up for a Vocalpoint survey, I want you to try at least one of the unconventional shopping methods mentioned in this chapter. Whichever you choose, I promise a new level of shopper satisfaction. If I'm wrong, send me a bill.   ✂

Resources

For Buying Coupons
eBay: www.ebay.com
PayPal: www.PayPal.com

For Previewing Coupons:
Sunday Coupon Preview: www.sundaycouponpreview.com

For Trading Coupons
Meetup: www.meetup.com
How to Shop for Free: www.howtoshopforfree.net

For Buying Gift Certificates
Card Pool: www.cardpool.com
Plastic Jungle: www.plasticjungle.com

For Free Promo and Discount Codes

Coupon Seven: www.couponseven.com

Ebates: www.ebates.com

Retail Me Not: www.retailmenot.com

Clipping Services

Coupon Clipping Crew: www.couponclippingcrew.com

Coupons & Things by Dede: www.couponsthingsbydede.com

The Coupon Cutters: www.thecouponcutters.com

The Coupon Master: www.thecouponmaster.com

Product Testing

All You Reality Checker: www.allyou.com

BzzAgent: www.bzzagent.com

House Party: www.houseparty.com

Kraft First Taste: www.kraftfirsttaste.com

Pssst: http://pssst.generalmills.com

Vocalpoint: www.vocalpoint.com

7

Scams, Cheats, and Big-Time Couponing No-Nos

I've said all along that I "play by the rules," so before we go any further I want to explain what it means to *not* play by the rules. That way, you'll feel confident that you're not breaking any. For starters, there's a difference between a hard-core extreme shopper, which is how I describe myself, and (kids, cover your ears) a dirty coupon ho (DCH). While I've been known to act a little crazy (recall the image of me guarding a mountain of clumping kitty litter while my kids retrieved three carriages), I never do anything illegal. A dirty coupon ho, on the other hand, will disregard the rules if they stand in the way of what she wants, creating a bad name for those of us who do things on the up-and-up.

What's in the cart?

Here's what you'll find in this chapter:
- Couponing: the difference between right and wrong
- Absolute shopping no-no's
- The consequences for bad behavior
- How to spot a dirty coupon scam

To be fair, before I go pointing the finger at those who play dirty, I have to admit that cheating the system was a temptation I consciously had to resist. When I first stumbled upon the secret society of couponers performing the dark arts—decoding, manipulating, photocopying, and even faking their own coupons to score more free stuff than would fit in their mini-vans—I was both disgusted and slightly aroused. Nothing captures my attention more than the word "free." Just ask my husband. When the man buys me flowers, I nag him for wasting money, but when he comes home with a stack of Sunday coupon inserts, I want to take him straight to bed.

Let's back up. When I was just learning how to shop for free, I'd spend hours and hours online researching coupons and educating myself on how to work the best deals. My family whined that I'd become obsessed, which wasn't entirely unfair, but saving money had become my mission. And a personal mission is one to be taken seriously—especially when the whole clan benefits—wouldn't you agree?

Soon enough (and quite innocently, I might add), I fell in through the back door to the online coupon underground. Here, naughty shoppers talk about how to bend and break the rules to amass free products. I sensed right away that this was not a place for me to spend my time, but on the other hand, I thought, *maybe knowing what not to do is as important as knowing what to do*? I justified that researching coupon abuse would broaden my continuing education.

For me, learning (and by that I mean gaining an understanding of, not practicing) how to manipulate the system was both scary and enlightening. I'd had no idea so much naughtiness existed. Not sure what to do with all the information I uncovered, I nervously blabbed about my online discovery to a few fellow shoppers. Big mistake. Before I could unhinge the wheels from their carts, they took the underground's dirty secrets to the stores and began overriding the system. In a court of law, this is illegal and called coupon fraud.

That some of my fellow shoppers were now candidates for criminal arrest didn't discourage them. Breaking the rules was fun, they told me. "And so easy, Kathy, you should totally try it," they said, like a teenager daring her law-abiding friend to shoplift. It didn't take long before stories started circulating in the Northeast about coupon abuse and how suspicious customers were being banned from stores. After an especially fraudulent transaction, a shopper was escorted out by the police, and in front of her children. I don't care what kind of deal you're getting—public humiliation in front of your kids is not worth it! I couldn't believe what some shoppers were risking just to get more for less when you can shop for free totally legally.

How you shop is up to you, of course, but since I learned the ugly truth about coupon fraud, I won't allow visitors to my site www.howtoshopforfree.net even to discuss it. It's simply not allowed. In my sandbox, either play nice, or get out.

The Difference Between Right and Wrong

Coupon fraud is when someone tries to redeem a coupon that is void, and often for a product that the shopper hasn't even purchased. In layman's terms, it's stealing. Experts estimate that coupon fraud costs the industry between $500 million and $800 million annually. That's a mega-loss that hurts both the stores and the manufacturers. In turn, it affects us—the honest consumers—because it eventually leads to an increase in store prices. Worst of all, the unscrupulous shoppers breaking the rules give the rest of us who are playing fair a bad name. I resent this. Thankfully, there are more of us than there are of them.

Nothing would sadden me more if manufacturers stopped issuing coupons or retailers stopped accepting them because a relatively small group of shady shoppers had exploited the system. I wrote this book to show people like you how to get more for less and how to go about getting it the "right" way. Everything you've read in these pages is completely legit. I've trained you to be one of the good girls, so relax. That said, while you're perfecting your shopping strategy, you're apt to make a mistake from time to time. That's okay. I don't want you to think that accidentally handing the cashier the wrong coupon will get you handcuffed. Most cashiers will just hand it back to you with a shake of the head and maybe a, "Better luck next time, sweetheart." Give yourself some latitude to mess up. Whoops moments are bound to happen.

You Asked It

Q: *Just to be sure I'm shopping for free without breaking the rules, what are the big no-no's? The things I should never do, even accidentally.*

A: *Mess-ups are one thing. Absolute no-no's are quite another. You'll find a list of absolute no-no's below, and a list of other bad behaviors on page 136.*

Absolute No-No's

- Decoding coupons with the intention of manipulating or overriding the system (See Hot Tip on the next page.)
- Using a coupon for anything other than the product, size, and/or quantity written on the coupon
- Scanning, reprinting, or photocopying coupons
- Using expired coupons (unless your store is specifically clear about accepting expired coupons)
- Modifying the coupon in any way, as in removing the expiration date, messing with the image, or changing the value of the coupon
- Using more than one manufacturer coupon per item
- Selling counterfeit coupons
- Creating counterfeit coupons
- Setting your computer to override a company's print-tracking software

If you have done any of the above, stop. You're committing coupon fraud and if you're caught, that awesome deal you got on three cases of Pellegrino water isn't going to seem so awesome anymore. And in addition, you're wrecking things for the rest of us who want to continue to play this shopping game fair and square. If you "didn't know" you were doing anything illegal, now you do. No more excuses. Stop acting like a dirty coupon ho.

HOT TIP: Don't Decode the Code

Every coupon has a 12-number barcode on it, called the Universal Product Code, and this number represents a coupon's secret language. For example, the code designed to speak to the store scanner might reveal what the dollar value of the coupon is, whether or not it doubles, who the manufacturer is, among other things. To decode a coupon is to break down and interpret what each number says about the coupon value. Those who decode are often the worst abusers of the system because they use this secret knowledge to override the system and manipulate store sales. Urban legend has it that a DCH once used a decoded K-Y Jelly coupon to purchase a whole roasted chicken. Not only is this downright unappetizing, it's coupon fraud. *Confused?* Not sure how a shopper would pick up dinner with a personal lubricant coupon? Good. I'm not going to teach you how to do it! My intention is only to give you a basic understanding of what decoding is. (Add it to your cache of cocktail party topics.) And really, all you need to know is that it's considered coupon fraud, which is a serious crime and totally N-O-T cool.   ✂

So now that you know what you can't do, I want to give you some examples of just downright bad behavior. The following actions won't get you fined or arrested, but making them your practice might earn you the label, "obnoxious coupon ho." *Note: I didn't make these scenarios up. They've either been reported to me, or I witnessed them first-hand.*

Bad Behavior

- Taking more than your share of coupons from a tear pad. How many is too many? The entire pad! After you've torn off two or three, walk away. Same goes for peelies. Don't strip an entire product line of its peelies.
- Clearing an entire shelf. Remember: Feel free to take a lot, but don't take it all. (Unless it's on clearance. In that case, feel free to ho it up.)
- Hiding a highly prized sale item at the back of a shelf or at the bottom of a full-priced bin, so that when it's marked down even further, it's MINE, MINE, MINE!
- Pushing shoppers out of the way so you can grab the last sale item.
- Snagging the last of a sale item out of someone else's cart. (I've seen it happen and it's ugly.)
- Belittling store cashiers who don't understand their own store policy. "Can you read?" and "Are you stupid?" are popular insults.
- Accepting a larger discount than you should because the "idiot cashier" (see above) messed up.
- Stealing coupons out of your neighbor's mail. (I think this probably constitutes illegal activity and should go in the no-no category.)

How to Spot a Scam

Now that we've gotten the big no-no's out of the way and I'm confident you won't knowingly pull anything over on any manufacturers or retailers, I want to make sure *you're* protected.

Checklist

How to Spot a Dirty Coupon

✓ **Check the Obvious.** Every coupon should say "manufacturer" or "store" coupon on it and show a valid remit address for the manufacturer. Every coupon should contain a bar code and an expiration date. If any of these details are missing, the coupon is probably dirty. Be suspicious.

✓ **Know Your Source.** Where did your coupons come from? Sites like SmartSource, RedPlum, Coupons.com, and any that I've mentioned throughout these pages are completely legit. There's no need to question the validity of a coupon from reputable and trusted sites. If, however, you've printed a coupon from a site or personal blog you're unfamiliar with or clipped it from a booklet you've never seen before, it might be worth your while to sniff around and make sure it's the real deal. *Note:* Just because it's on the Internet doesn't make it authentic. When in doubt, look it up on the Coupon Information Corporation (CIC) website, www.cents-off.com.

✓ **Print Limits.** If you receive a PDF coupon via e-mail, pay attention to the source and what the coupon is for. Is the value unbelievably awesome? Is the coupon hard to read? Any PDF coupon with a smudged barcode, unusual wording, or blurry imagery is likely to be a fake that has been photocopied and spread across the Internet. Any PDF coupon that you can print unlimited copies of is most likely a fake. Most manufacturers will not issue coupons that have no print limits. They're not stupid.

✓ **If It Sounds Too Good to Be True, It Probably Is.** Printable coupons for 100 percent off (that is, FREE stuff) are usually fake. I wish I could say differently, but I can't. Sometimes manufacturers will issue coupons for a free product with no purchase required, but these gems usually come in the mail and are sent directly from the MFR. If you're at all suspicious, check the manufacturer website before you try and use it.

SHOPPER'S HALL OF SHAME
Using Fake Coupons

"About a year ago I told my two elderly aunts (down in the deep south) that I was couponing for a living, and they started bragging about all these things they were getting for free from coupons they found on the Internet. Every day they'd print out their handful and go over to Walmart to get their free stuff: aluminum foil, laundry soap, and tons of food items. Well, I did some research online and found out that the coupons they were printing were fraudulent copies that were YEARS old—coupons that originated in the '80s but had no expiration date on them. I had to call my poor aunts and tell them that they had essentially stolen all that merchandise. They were mortified and asked if they should take their items back. At the time I had no clue, but I called their Walmart store and spoke with a super nice manager who totally understood the situation. He let them keep everything as a "reward" for letting him know about the bad coupons. Apparently there were dozens of other people in their small town who were using the same coupons, and, by being honest, we saved his store from a huge profit loss."

Brenda, Clinton, Massachusetts

Checklist
How to Spot a Dirty Coupon Scam

✓ **Coupon Books.** Beware of the bogus entrepreneurs selling so-called coupon books. It's a scam. Here's how they dupe you: Scammers promise that if you buy their coupon books at a discounted price, you can make "thousands per month" by reselling the coupons. Not true. Watch out for:
  - Guarantees of big profits, high income or amazing savings in a short time
  - Claims that no risk is involved
  - Pressure to act now
  - Claims that this is a hot, "can't miss" opportunity

✓ **Clipping Services.** Beware of websites promising, "Earn hundreds of dollars each week clipping coupons!" Websites that promise amazing profits to those who clip coupons out of newspapers and magazines and send them to a clipping service are just scamming you. Don't fall for it.

Consequences for Playing Dirty

According to the Coupon Information Corporation (CIC), a not-for-profit association dedicated to enhancing the integrity of the coupon-redemption process, penalties for those convicted of coupon fraud vary, but financial penalties in the ballpark of $200,000 and prison sentences of between three and five years are not uncommon. The longest prison sentence on file for coupon fraud is seventeen years. *Are you kidding me?* I love a bargain, but nothing's worth doing time.

Stopping Fraud

Not only is the CIC watching you, but manufacturers and retailers are getting smart. The *Wall Street Journal* has reported that some food makers have taken aggressive steps to stop the redemption of counterfeit coupons. General Mills, Inc., has begun including holograms on some of its coupons. Hormel Foods has also begun putting holograms and watermarks on some coupons it distributes through newspaper circulars. SmartSource.com has included a hidden marking on its coupons that changes every month. The site has also created a new font that can't be easily loaded onto users' computers and will later add microscopic type along the edge of the coupon that lists the expiration date or a repeated message. The big dogs are on your scent, so if you're playing dirty, you better clean up your act.

Busted!

I know this chapter is a bit of a party pooper, but I had to level with you. I want you to be safe and stay out of trouble. And not to belabor the point (but I am a mother and that's what we do), before we move on to the next chapter, I think it's important I provide you with some very real stories from the coupon underground to drive home the message that playing dirty isn't worth it.

- 2010: A woman from Brooksville, Florida, admitted to stealing thirty-six $10-off coupons from the Publix where she worked as a cashier. She converted the coupons into $360 in cash. This DCH was charged with grand theft.
- 2010: Portland, Oregon, police are building a case against a woman accused of using fake coupons to stockpile an obscene amount of stuff. This DCH printed counterfeit coupons to score big at stores like Kohl's and Safeway. Sometimes, she'd return the stolen goods in exchange for gift cards.
- 2009: A man from Clarksburg, Maryland, was arrested and charged with theft for using expired and altered coupons for purchases at Target. His dirty tricks resulted in a loss of $8,000 to the store.

- 2008: A woman from O'Fallon, Missouri, was charged with fourteen counts of felony forgery. This DCH collected legitimate, high-value MFR coupons and scanned them on her home computer. She purchased new products with the fakes and then resold them at garage sales for profit and on eBay, where her member name was "onlyway2shop." But there *is* another way. If only she'd known how to shop for free legally, she'd still be on the outside trading coupons instead of trading cigarettes in the slammer. Sorry, low blow.

Enough of the rap sheet. Let's move on. All this talk of coupon abuse puts me in a foul mood. Let's get back into the stores and shop for free. That always cheers me up. Next, I'll show you how to score high-value coupons for organic products. Are you into it?

Resources
To report coupon abuse, contact the Coupon Information Corporation (CIC), www.cents-off.com.

8

Eat Healthy on the Super Cheap

By now, I hope I've convinced you that shopping for free really is possible, but I've found that even my hard-won bargainistas have a really hard time digesting my claim that I get meat, fresh veggies, and organic food for free. They assume that because I stockpile beef franks and chocolate pudding, that that's all I feed my family. Please, I may not be a total locavore, but I lean green. But it's the disbelievers who keep me motivated and at the top of my shopping game. Their skepticism has made me a smarter and savvier shopper—always on the quest for healthier, tastier, and yet still, free food for my family. Free fresh meat, produce, and organic food can be tough to find. I admit it. But that doesn't mean it's not possible.

What's in the cart?

Here's what you'll find in this chapter:
- Score fresh chicken, fish, and beef with wine tags
- Get milk and dairy with overage dollars
- Make money on Catalina deals

- Find fruit on the super cheap in the produce department
- Get your hands on high-value coupons for organic products

Fresh Meat

Fresh meat is often the biggest hog of our grocery store dollars, so let's tackle it first. (Unless, of course, you're a vegetarian. In that case, you might want to skip ahead to Organic for Free toward the end of the chapter.) The question I probably get asked more than any other on my website, www.howtoshopforfree.net, is, how, pray tell, do you get fresh chicken and strip steak for free? I tend to go about in one of three ways.

Overage Dollars

Sometimes you'll find deals where you can make money. We call this "overage," or "a money maker," and you can use this bonus money toward other items on your shopping list. For example, check out this money maker:

Starkist tuna sale price	– $1.79
Store coupon	– $1.00 off
MFR coupon	– $1.00 off
OVERAGE	= $0.21

It's only twenty-one cents, but do this with enough items and the overage adds up. Typically, accumulated overage is what I use to buy fresh meat and produce.

Another example:

Special K cereal is on sale for $1 a box. You have a manufacturer coupon for $5 off of four boxes. You purchase four boxes for $4, and, with the coupon, you end up with a dollar in overage. This deal is a money maker. Here's another one:

Cottage cheese sale price	$1.49
Store coupon	$1 off
Manufacturer coupon	$1 off
OVERAGE	= $0.51 cents Money Maker!

Note: Overage dollars are not handed back to you at the end of your transaction like change. They work like credit toward other items on your grocery bill. In the example above, the fifty-one cents in overage would count toward, or take fifty-one cents off, another item in your cart. Make sense?

I use this overage money to buy chicken breasts and fresh seafood (or any other pricey item in the store). Of course, even when it's on sale, good meat isn't cheap, so overage dollars only get me so far.

Wine Tags

The second way I score my favorite barbecue delights for free is by using the coupons found on wine tags. Wine tags are manufacturer coupon "tags" attached to bottles. They're not on every bottle, so you have to look around, but believe me, it's worth the search. Wine tags specifically offer big savings on meat, seafood, specialty cheeses, fruit, and produce. The last time I cruised the wine aisles, I grabbed a wine tag that gave me $3.00 off a turkey (with no specifications on what type of turkey), so I picked up a package of ground turkey that was on sale for $2.99 making it totally free. I've gotten the same kind of deals with ham. A $5-off ham wine tag can be used to get a small ham or sliced ham. Does this mean you have to stock up on wine in order to shop for smoked chicken breast for free? The answer is no, but if you're buying wine anyway, look for a bottle with a tag on it. Most tags say, *wine purchase required*, but many do not. You may have to do a little hunting around, but they can be found. This is when your shopping buddy comes in handy. You can cover the wine department as a team, get the job done faster and share the profits.

The trick with wine tags is to get only the amount of meat that will make it free, or nearly free. Pay attention to your weight. I often separate my orders to get chicken, beef, and seafood for free. For example, let's say I have four wine tags for $1 off *any* seafood. I'll go to the fish counter and see what's on sale for $4 a pound, and then I'll order a quarter of a pound of four separate items. Why separate items? Because that way, I can use my four coupons, applying one to each quarter pound order. Here's how to work it:

Fresh shrimp $3.99/lb = $0.99 for a ¼ lb
Fresh perch $3.99/lb = $0.99 for a ¼ lb
Fresh scallops $3.99/lb = $0.99 for a ¼ lb
Fresh haddock $3.99/lb = $0.99 for a ¼ lb

Not a ton of fish, but enough to make a great scampi, seafood casserole, or gumbo. And it's totally on the house!

HOT TIP: Peel off a Nice Slice of Meat
In addition to hunting wine tags, when you're at the deli and meat counter, keep your eyes peeled for "peelies,"—remember, those are the coupons stuck on packages that you peel off. I often get a huge break on Perdue chicken breasts, cutlets, and chicken fingers when I apply a peelie toward a store sale. Plus, if you get your hands on a store-issued peelie, you can combine it with a manufacturer wine tag for a double-score discount. A $2-off peelie combined with a $2-off wine tag can go a long way with chicken.

Here's another one: Steak tips were selling at my local grocer for $4.99 a pound. I rang the buzzer and asked the butcher to please give me four quarter-pound packages of steak tips. (Most butchers will happily do this, so don't be afraid to ask.) My quarter-pound packages totaled $1.25, and I used a $1-off coupon on each, bringing my cost down to $0.25 per package. The steak tips that were priced at $4.99 a pound, I got for a $1.00 a pound. That's one heck of a deal for marinated steak.

You Asked It

Q: *Isn't taking the wine tags without the wine considered stealing, or just bad behavior?*

A: *It's absolutely not stealing. Bad behavior? That's your call. I have no problem slipping tags off their bottles and going on my merry way, but if you feel awkward doing this, don't do it. Just know this: People who design marketing promotions (and that's what a wine tag is) are very good at what they do. If they want you to purchase the wine, they will say so. Most of the time, the wine bottle is simply being used as the "messenger"— a delivery system, if you will—to get a coupon into the hands of a customer in a particular zip code (that's you!). The manufacturer doing the promotion (Hormel, Cracker Barrel, etc.) doesn't care if you buy the wine. They only care that you buy* their *product. What you shouldn't do (DCH alert) is swipe all the tags in the vicinity.*

Catalina Deals

To those of you who don't live within walking or driving distance to a store with Catalina deals, my heart goes out to you because, truly, I live for these deals. For those of you who don't know what a "Catalina" or a "CAT" is, let me enlighten you: In simple terms, "Catalina" refers to a Catalina (brand name) machine that sits right next to the cash register in many grocery stores. After you pay for your groceries, this machine will often spit out "CATs," also known as "check-out coupons," "register rewards," or "store money." Whether or not you get a CAT is determined by your store purchases.

Most CATs are MFR coupons (usually for something you just bought) good on your next shopping trip. But other times, a CAT will say something like, *Take $5 off your next shopping order*, and you know what that means—you've just been handed cash. These are the CATs I go after like a lioness in heat.

The manufacturers who concoct these crazy Catalina deals include ConAgra Foods, Unilever, Procter & Gamble, Kraft Foods, and General Mills. Their hope is that by providing you with a cash incentive, you'll try a number of their products, become familiar with their brand, and (fingers crossed) get hooked on their goods and come back for more.

You probably run across Catalina deals without even realizing it. A store ad in the paper or promotional sign in your local grocery store will advertise a deal like, *Buy FIVE of these items and get $10 off your next order! Or, Spend $25 on these items and get $10 back.* Make a mental note: These are Catalina deals. The must-buy items could be anything from ice cream, tuna fish, or ketchup to diapers, and they very well might not be things you necessarily need or want, so you skip it. Big mistake! Ladies, these might not look like deals, but if you work them right, you can make a lot of money cashing in on these sales. For example, during one particularly good Catalina week, I brought home over $1,800 of groceries for free and made money in the process. True story. I get goose bumps now just thinking about it.

Catalinas take some upfront planning and strategizing, but they totally pay off. Let me show you how to work the first kind of deal: *Buy FIVE of these items and get $10 off your next order.*

Not too long ago, a CAT deal of this kind included Pringles chips on the list of items. After doing my homework, I discovered they were on sale for $1. Seriously, who did the math on this deal? It wasn't very smart on the store's part, but it was going to work out great for me, so I went for it. I bought five cans of Pringles for $5, and the store gave me $10 back. That's a $5 money maker. I did this over and over again until I couldn't stand the sight of one more can of Pringles, and I was up $100. (I was the only lady handing out cans of Pringles to the neighborhood kids for Halloween that year.)

Rolling my money from one order into the next (called "rolling CATs" in this case) is how I get pork tenderloin and things like my husband's beloved beer, for which coupons aren't typically printed or sent, for free. When you see these deals advertised, take a minute to do the math and look for ways to work it. Looking again at the scenario above, let's say that the Pringles were $2 a can and I bought five. I would have spent $10 and gotten $10 back, making the chips totally free. Or if Pringles were $3 a can and I bought five for $15, and used five MFR coupons for $1 off a can, I'd still get them for free. A great deal, either way!

Now let's consider this deal: *Spend $25 on these items and get $10 back.* As soon as a CAT like this is advertised, I go into super-strategy mode. I know if I work it right, I could roll a lot of do-re-mi. First, I go to the store and price out the featured items. What most people don't know is that, *shhhhhhhhhh*, Catalinas are based on the pre-sale price, not the advertised sale price. If the pre-sale price of Crest or Tom's of Maine toothpaste is $3.69 and it's on sale for $1.79, it's the pre-sale price of $3.69 that will be counted toward your total dollars spent, even though you're only paying $1.79. Plus, if you throw a $1-off coupon on top of that, now you're only spending $0.79, but $3.69 is still going toward your total sale. Not sure you get it?

Check it out:

Spend $25, Get $10 Back
Crest toothpaste $3.69 presale, $1.79 on sale
Note: The presale and sale prices are both listed on the shelf tag.

I will buy seven and this will total out to $25.83, even though I will only be spending $12.53.

Seven Crest toothpaste @$3.69 = $25.83 presale
Seven Crest toothpaste @$1.79 = $12.53 on sale

So far, I've spent $12.53. I have seven coupons for $1 off, so . . .

$12.53 sale price
− $7.00 in coupons
= $5.23 total dollars spent.
But then, the store gives me $10 back and now I'm up $4.77

This kind of CAT has at least nine lives. I can roll it over and over again until I run out of coupons or the store runs out of toothpaste, whichever comes first. If I do this ten times, I will be up $47.77, which I can use to buy delicious steaks, fresh produce, and a bottle of bubbly or micro-brew for my hubby and me for a toast when I tell him how little I spent on groceries for the week. Is this illegal? Nope. It sounds too good to be true, doesn't it? These are the deals that make me lose sleep. Truly, I've been known to lie awake at night going over the numbers (out loud and sometimes to the point of waking up my poor husband) and sprinting out of bed in the morning so I can get to the store as early as possible. There have been times I've considered leaving my kids on the side of the road so that I could fit more free stuff into my SUV. You think I'm crazy? A little obsessed? Roll a few CATs, and then we'll talk.

On another CAT Extravaganza, I rolled a *Spend $30, Get $15 Back* Catalina deal and took home eighty cartons of free Breyers ice cream and made $76.44 in the process. Admittedly, eighty cartons of ice cream is a mountain of ice cream, even if you have a deep freezer like I do and four kids who love a sugar high. But because I could

---

SHOPPER'S
Hall of Fame

"My biggest savings come from Catalina sales. Catalina sales are initially confusing, especially if there is more than one going on at a time. It took me a few times to get the hang of it, but by my second Catalina sale, I was off and running! My personal record for a CAT sale is taking home $1,200 worth of products that I only paid $60 for (and I even made a few mistakes on that one). That is a 95 percent savings. I recommend starting small and preplanning your trips. Also, if you have a more seasoned couponer in your area, ask if you can tag along with her and watch. Sometimes seeing how it works makes it click."

Momma Bryant, Randolph, Maine

"buy" it without spending any real money out of pocket, I took it as a service to the neighborhood. At the end of my shopping spree, I went door-to-door giving away ice cream. I remember knocking on doors at nine-thirty at night, worried my neighbors would think I'd lost my mind, but since we were in the middle of a hot and muggy summer, they were happy to take it off my hands. I mean really, who doesn't want free ice cream in August?

You Asked It

Q: *Can I use Catalina dollars right away? Or do I have to wait until my next visit to the store?*

A: *You can "roll a CAT" a few different ways depending on your comfort level. Since we've already established that I'm more brazen than most, I'm sure you won't be surprised to learn that on a good Catalina week, I fill my carriage with three sets of CATs at one time. At the register, I put one order on the belt, separate it with a plastic divider from the next order, and separate that one from the third. When my first set of CATs print out, I use them to pay for order #2 and with the CATs from order #2, I pay for order #3. I take my loot to the car and head back into the store and do it all over again. This is how to hard-core roll it, girls! Someone with a little more self-control would likely buy one order, take it to the car, go back in, and try it with a different cashier. Or you might buy an order on Monday, go back on Tuesday, and so on throughout the sale week. It's really up to you and your chutzpah.*

The money I make working Catalina deals is the number one way I get fresh poultry, pork, and beef for free, and I highly encourage you to give it a try. I have a personal "Won't-Pay-More-For" policy, and this helps me keep my spending on meat and seafood low. These prices are based on deals I've gotten in the past, so I know they're out there, and I refuse to buy it (i.e., use my CATs) unless I can bag it for that price.

For example, I won't pay more than:

$1.99/lb for roast beef

$0.99/lb for ground beef

$3.99/lb for steak and steak tips

HOT TIP: Look for a 50 Percent Difference
Spend $20, Get $10 Back or *Spend $30, Get $15 Back* are the best Catalina deals because they offer you a huge opportunity to make money. Before you factor in the pre-sale price and add coupons to the deal, you're already getting 50 percent of your money back. ✂

$0.99/lb for boneless chicken breast
$0.69/lb for whole chickens
$0.59/lb for drumsticks and thighs
$0.99/lb for ground turkey
$0.99 to $1.50/lb for pork (depending on the cut)
$1.99/lb for sausage

I won't pay more for deli items than:
$3.99/lb for roast beef
$2.99/lb for turkey
$1.99 to $2.99/lb for ham
$1.99/lb for cheese

If you haven't already done so, get to know your meat prices in the different stores you shop and make friends with the butchers while

---

HOT TIP: Round Up the CATs

Generally the shoppers using the self-checkout lanes are in a hurry and not big on coupons. So while you're checking out in the standard I-have-a-lot-of-loot aisle, take a peek over at the self-checkout registers. Often, you'll notice these hasty shoppers rush off before the Catalina coupons even print. Sometimes even, they knowingly leave them behind or crumple them up and toss them in the trash! *Where's the respect?* The way I see it, this is abandoned money that needs a home. I've been known to send my antsy-pants kids over to self-checkouts to quickly sweep the Catalina machines while I'm checking out. If a CAT's been left behind, they've been instructed by Mommy to pocket it.   ✂

you're at it. A good friend at the meat counter will often clue you in to the best deals and point you toward big markdowns on meat that's about to expire. This is called a "loss leader" because stores know they'll probably lose money by putting items on sale for such a low price. (Their hope is that while you're saving big in the meat department, you'll spend frivolously in another section. Ha! Not me.)

On the basis of what I've learned from butchers over the years, I often buy meat that's close to its expiration date and throw it right into the freezer. Generally this meat is no older than other meat you buy in the store; the store just happens to have more of it and needs to move product. Freezing meat immediately stops the aging process. Then when I'm ready to cook it, I remove it from the freezer, and it's good to go. Remember: This meat is great meat; your store is simply concerned it won't move its inventory in time.

When I was still learning how to shop for free, I'd stock up on meat whenever I came across good deals, and this is what I recommend to you. As you're getting the hang of rolling CATs and using wine tags to get pastrami for free, focus on getting as much high-quality meat as you can for low, low prices. When you spot a good deal—take it all and throw it into the freezer. Remember, it all goes back to stockpiling the deals when you can get them. Once your freezer is stocked, you can return your focus to only getting it when it's free, or nearly free.

Milk and Dairy

Believe it or not, loading up on dairy products for free is easy. Coupons for milk, cream, butter, sour cream, cream cheese, yogurt, and cheeses can be found regularly online, in store circulars, and in the paper. Pair a coupon with a store sale, and dairy easily works out for free. Organic milk companies often put out high-value coupons, and I pair them with a sale to get organic milk for free.

HOT TIP: Hit the Meat Market

Another smart way to get meat for low prices is to shop at a
local butcher shop. Many independent butchers are realizing
that in order to compete with BOGO deals and other big
manufacturer sales on meat, they have to lower their prices. If
you find a great per pound price at your local butcher shop,
buy in bulk and stock up.   ✂

Most stores have a reduced dairy section, like with meats, where
items are marked down because they're close to their expiration date.
I've been known to load up on creamer and milk for free this way.
For example, I found cartons of Oakhurst Half and Half in the
reduced section because they were close to the expiration date. (BTW:
The general consensus is that dairy is good for one week past its
expiration date.) The cartons were marked down to $1, and I had
$2-off/2 coupons, so I got four of them for free, and I cooked a seafood
casserole with them that night. Not all four containers of cream in
one casserole! Surely you know me better. I made one for dinner and
two more that I threw in the freezer for nights down the road when
I'm not in the mood to cook.

I've gotten sour cream similarly:

Sour cream on sale for $1.49
Minus $0.75-off coupon that doubles to $1.50
TOTAL = FREE

If you're not going to use it right away, don't be afraid to throw
milk in the freezer. It'll keep for about a month that way. Simply thaw
it out in the fridge when you're ready to use it. (Smaller containers

work best when freezing milk.) As for other basics in the dairy department, you heard it here: You can always get butter and margarine for free, and you can freeze them, as well. I currently have eight tubs of Smart Balance buttery spread stashed away in my freezer. I know—that's a lot, but it was free, and eventually we will use it all.

In addition to wine tags, coupons for specialty cheeses can often be found around the deli area. Start looking around. Once you train your eye to spot savings, you'll notice they're all around you. Like with anything else, when you see a good deal on cheese, load up. And like butter, quality cheese can be frozen. (Hard and shredded cheeses work best in colder climates.) Simply wrap them tight and they'll keep for up to four months in your freezer. If I don't find good store sales to match with coupons in a given week, I get the dairy products I need with overage. As I mentioned earlier, I frequently get milk at CVS with Extra Care Bucks. Remember the last time you ran out of milk and ended up at a convenience store? Maybe it was a holiday eve and the market was closed—wouldn't it have been nice to get that gallon for free?

Fruits and Vegetables

Granted, they're few and far between, but coupons for fresh fruit do exist. For example, Kellogg's often has a coupon that gives you money off your favorite fruit when you buy two boxes of Special K. If you have coupons to get the Special K for free, then you can get both the fruit and the cereal for free. Typically, I buy fruit with overage money or after rolling CATs and I shop in the following areas of the store for the best deals.

Check the Markdown Rack

Almost every grocery store has a markdown rack of produce. Similar to meat and dairy nearing its expiration date, fruit on the markdown section is starting to get spots or go soft. You can almost always find bananas on the markdown rack. I scoop these up because I know my family of six will easily go through them before they turn, and if not, I chop them up and throw them in the freezer for smoothies. Many of us wrongly reject fruits that have small bruises or spots on them. Shoppers, this is fruit that is still delicious and edible, but that the store is about to throw out in the trash because they may have taken more than they could sell into inventory. You can cut this fruit up, toss the parts that are bruised, and cook with or freeze the rest. Use your head! Just the other day, I got ten bananas for 33 cents. Major score for me, and the store loved it, too. I saved someone a ride to the dumpster. I'm like a green super hero.

Buy Frozen

As for produce, you can always get frozen veggies for free. With a $0.50 coupon that you can double, there's always something on sale for $1, and then it's free. A bonus with frozen veggies is that they tend to have less salt and sugar than the canned versions. I look for frozen veggies with no other ingredient than the vegetable. For example, a bag of frozen corn should list the ingredients as "corn." That's all. These veggies were frozen at their peak of goodness and will taste just as yummy when you decide to thaw and eat them.

Think Seasonally

Scoring fresh, *free* produce is a little more tricky, but not impossible As with fruit, I tend to get my fresh veggies with overage money after rolling CATs and I only buy what's in season and on sale. For example, throughout the summer months I can always find killer deals on corn, green beans, and yellow squash in my local grocery stores. When I spot a sale like twelve ears of corn for a buck, for example, I stock up. What my family can't eat, I husk and freeze. I do similarly with zucchini and squash. What we don't eat right away, I use in a veggie lasagna or a minestrone soup and freeze.

Most of us are so used to buying whatever we want (mango and avocado!) when we want it (right now!), we haven't paid much attention to what fruits and vegetables are native to our area and when they're at the peak of their season. Native produce + peak of the season = lowest price. I love a fresh mango, but the last time I checked, they don't grow in Massachusetts, so I'm going to pay out the wazoo to have my mango craving satisfied. I'm better off eating strawberries, which grow like weeds where I live and are considerably cheaper than other fruits. Once you become aware of what's growing in your region and let what's in season dictate what produce you buy, you'll automatically start saving money.

Grow Your Own

Other than picking up local produce with overage bucks, the best way I know how to get free, fresh produce is to grow your own. If you grow it, then you're not buying it, right? Plus, if you buy your plants off-season like I do, you can get fruit trees for up to 75 percent off. I've found some great deals on Craig's List, and Lowe's and Home Depot have great sidewalk sales. One year, my husband and I planted five apple, two peach, and two cherry trees; six blueberry, strawberry, and blackberry bushes; and a raspberry plant. We have two vegetable gardens where we've planted leaf lettuce, red onions, sweet peppers, asparagus, eggplant, potatoes, cucumbers, green beans, squash, zucchini, broccoli, and eight varieties of tomatoes. We even grow our own herbs (not that kind). Since I've gone back to nature, so to speak, I've been happy to discover that other gardeners like to share their crops. I often get fresh flowers and heirloom veggies this way, and in turn, I give a lot away. I realize that not everyone has the space or the time for a garden, so I'll show you how to do the next best thing— shop organic for free.

Organic for Free

Many natural and organic food companies have hopped on the coupon bandwagon, but because many of your favorite natural foods are packaged by small companies without big budgeting dollars for printed coupon circulation, it's not in the newspapers, but online where you'll find the best deals.

Believe it or not, I often find discounts on organic food on the big coupon sites like www.print.coupons.com and www.coupons.smartsource.com, and I take full advantage. Right now, I have a fridge full of sixty Oikos Greek yogurts by Stonyfield Farms. And yes, I will eat it all. Stonyfield Farms regularly puts out a $1-off coupon for Oikos Greek yogurt, and one of my local grocery stores always has it on sale for $1, making it free. This is a perfect example of how I eat healthier because I shop for free. Before I started shopping like I do, I was never a big yogurt eater, but now I'm addicted to Greek yogurt. It has practically no fat. It's smooth, delicious, and it doubles as sour cream.

While you can often find coupons for organic and healthy food on sites like www.coupons.smartsource.com, an even better bet is to go directly to your favorite brand or product websites, like Organic Valley and Seventh Generation (see Resources for URLs), to maximize savings. Whatever you eat a lot of or have brand loyalty to, go to the company website and see what savings are available. Or do a general Internet search for "specific brand name + printable coupon" and see what comes up. If the company doesn't offer coupons online, use the contact information to e-mail a request for a coupon or a sample, and it doesn't hurt to say how much you love their product. I've gotten a lot of free stuff this way. You can also seek out websites dedicated to organic brands, like Mambo Sprouts, HealthESavers, and Hain Celestial, to see if they issue coupons directly from their sites, by mail, or at retailers' locations.

Of course, natural foods retailers are also getting into the game: Did you know that Whole Foods Market puts out a newsletter every month called the Whole Deal, which contains great info on savings, including high-value printable coupons? If you don't have a Whole Foods Market in your area, don't despair. Many smaller health food stores offer incentives, too, so start looking around and stop perpetuating the myth that all coupons are for junk!

Resources
The following natural foods and organic-friendly companies offer printable coupons and awesome deals when you visit their websites, sign up for their newsletters, become a fan on Facebook, or follow them on Twitter.

Arrowhead Mills: www.arrowheadmills.com (gluten free products)

Bear Naked: www.bearnaked.com (grain-ola bars)

Birds Eye: www.birdseyefoods.com (frozen veggies)

Brown Cow: www.browncowfarm.com (yogurt)

Cascadian Farms: www.cascadianfarm.com (organic granola and cereals)

Coleman Natural Foods: www.colemannatural.com (natural meats)

Dreamfields Foods: www.dreamfieldsfoods.com (healthy pastas)

Earthbound Farm: www.ebfarm.com (organic greens and fruit)

Earth's Best: www.earthsbest.com (organic baby foods)

Eden Foods: www.edenfoods.com (nuts and grains)

Heartland Pasta: www.heartlandpasta.com (whole wheat pastas)

Horizon Organic: www.horizondairy.com (milk and other things creamy)

Imagine Foods: www.imaginefoods.com (soups and stocks)

Kashi: www.kashi.com (cereal, crackers, cookies, and more)

Lightlife: www.lightlife.com (healthy hot dogs)

Mrs. Meyer's Clean Day: www.mrsmeyers.com (super clean cleaning supplies)

Muir Glen: www.muirglen.com (tomato saucy products)

Organic Valley: www.organicvalley.coop (organic milk)

Naked Juice: www.nakedjuice.com (just juice)

Nature's Path Foods: www.naturespath.com (crunchilicious cereal)

Nature's Way: www.naturesway.com (vitamins and homeopathic helpers)

Newman's Own Organics: www.newmansownorganics.com (coffee, snacks, and pet food)

Pearl Soymilk: www.pearlsoymilk.com (soy milk)

R.W. Knudsen: www.rwknudsenfamily.com (not just juice anymore)

Santa Cruz Organic: www.scojuice.com (organic juice)

Seventh Generation: www.seventhgeneration.com (cleaning supplies with a conscience)

Simply Organic: www.simplyorganicfoods.com (dips, dressings, and sauces)

Stonyfield Farms: www.stonyfield.com (Greek yogurt)

Tribe Mediterranean Foods: www.tribehummus.com (hummus)

Wild Harvest Organic: www.wildharvestorganic.com (healthy snack foods)

Additionally, check out these major websites for printing coupons from a variety of organic and natural brands:

Hain Celestial Group: www.hain-celestial.com

HealthESavers: www.healthesavers.com

Mambo Sprouts: www.mambosprouts.com

9

You're Covered: From Diapers to Drugs

So now that you're shopping for meat, produce, and organic goodies for free—is there anything you cannot do? I don't think so. Clearly, you're a shopping super star, and I'd be honored to share the grocery store aisles with you anytime. Because it's obvious you're taking this shopping game seriously, I think it's time I pass on a couple of my top-level shopping strategies. And by the way, I don't share this information with just simple amateurs.

What's in the Cart?

Here's what you'll find in this chapter:
- How to afford the basics for your baby's first year (diapers, wipes, formula, and gear—all free!)
- The secret to staying healthy without going broke
- How to lower your co-pay by switching pharmacies
- Where to score prescription drugs for free

You're Pregnant, Now What?

I don't care what your household income is, babies are expensive. The diapers, wipes, creams, formula, bedding, and binkies—*ahhhhh!* If you've had a baby, you know what I'm talking about. When I was a new, young mother, I worried endlessly over how I was going to stretch my budget to buy everything I needed to keep my baby girl and me alive, but I was uninformed. Now I know better, and I'm going to pass all that I've learned on to you. By combining sales with coupons, signing up for e-newsletters, and becoming a member on key websites, you can get many of the essentials that go along with having a baby for free.

Diapers

Before I found the holy shopping grail, my three oldest kids got the cheapest diapers I could find—you know the ones that on a particularly bad day can't handle the job? Even cheap and flimsy,

---

HOT TIP: Score Free Baby Swag

Moms (and I'm not just talking about moms in the low-income bracket, but *all* moms) are eligible for tons of cool, free services. For example, did you know that your local fire or police station will install your car seat for you as a simple good will gesture? And that your health insurance company will send you a baby starter-kit, along with generous gifts like your first Baby Book just for asking? No—you're not hallucinating from sleep deprivation. You read that sentence right. Your insurance company wants to give you a hand, so reach out and take it, woman.   ✂

---

diapers are still a huge expense, and I cursed the frequency with which I had to buy them. I thought, "I'm going to go broke just keeping their little butts clean and covered." By the time my fourth came along, who is now four and the last of the litter, I'd discovered the secret to shopping for free, and I never had to buy a single diaper for that kid. Follow these simple guidelines and you, too, will keep your babies covered for free.

 Checklist

Shopping for Diapers for Free

✓ Remember what I told you about brand loyalty? If you want to score free diapers, you must throw brand loyalty out with the bath water.

✓ Only shop for diapers that are on sale or better yet, on clearance. Marked-down diapers mean more savings when you apply your bargainista know-how.

✓ Buy the smallest package at the lowest price.

✓ Apply your high-value coupons to smaller packages to bring the cost down even lower. Instead of buying in bulk, buy multiples.

✓ Pay the remaining balance with Extra Care Bucks at CVS, Register Rewards at Walgreens, or with CATs at your grocery store.

✓ Stockpile. But don't go nuts. If you stockpile too many newborn size diapers, your baby may be walking before you use them all.

The following three shopping strategies are typically how I score diapers for free. I encourage you to keep your eyes and ears open for opportunities like the ones described below and be ready to hit the stores.

Shopping Strategy #1: The Catalina Deal
Who knew CATs and diapers would go so well together?

```
CATALINA Spend $40, get $20
Remember: CATs are triggered based on the pre-sale price
Pampers presale price = $13.99 x 3      = $41.97
Pampers sale price = $8.99 x 3          = $26.97
Apply three $2.00-off coupons            − $6.00
SUBTOTAL                                = $20.97
```

I buy three packs to bring my total to $41.97, even though in reality I'm only spending $26.97 out of pocket. I use three $2.00-off MFR coupons and now I'm only spending $20.97. I throw a store printable for $1.00-off/1 into the mix, and now my total out of pocket cost is $20, and the store gives me $20 back in CATs. My three packs of Pampers are FREE. Meow!

```
$20 OOP (out of pocket)
$20 back in CATs
TOTAL = FREE
```

Shopping Strategy #2: CVS—Extra Care Bucks
By applying your hard-won sleuthing skills ahead of time, you can make a killing at CVS in the diaper aisle.

I notice in the CVS store circular that Pampers are on sale for *$7.99, receive $5.00 in ECBs*. Remember: ECBs work like cash.

I know that by combining ECB deals, I can work this Pampers sale to my full advantage. Check it out:

At the same time they're having the Pampers deal, CVS has a promotion such that when you purchase a bottle of Excedrin for $1.99, you get $1.99 back in ECBs. Okay—now we're in business. I use an MFR coupon for $2.00-off any bottle of Excedrin. I spend nothing out of pocket, and I'm up $1.99 on the deal.

Then, I purchase one package of Pampers and use a $1.00-off MFR coupon to bring the total owed to $6.99. I throw in the $1.99 ECBs from my Excedrin purchase and now my out of pocket cost is five dollars. I pay the five bucks and receive five back in Extra Care Bucks. The Pampers are FREE.

Pampers on sale	$7.99
Apply MFR coupon	− $1.00
SUBTOTAL	= $6.99
Use ECBs from Excedrin deal	− $1.99
TOTAL	= $5.00
Receive $5 back in ECBs	

Shopping Strategy #3: Rite Aid—Use a Gift Card

By transferring a prescription from another pharmacy, Rite Aid will "reward" you with a loaded gift card that you can use to load up on diapers.

I fill a new medical prescription at the Rite Aid pharmacy and receive a $25.00 gift card to use on anything in the store. I wait until Rite Aid brand diapers are marked down from 50 to 75 percent off. (Note: when diapers go on clearance, I suspend my rule: *Take a lot, but don't take it all*. When they're this cheap, I follow a different rule: *Finders, Keepers*.) I purchase six packages at $3.50 a piece for a total of $21.00. I use a Rite Aid $5-off of $20 coupon and now my total is $16.00.

Rite Aid brand diapers $3.50 x 6	= $21.00
Use a $5 off $20 coupon	− $5.00
SUBTOTAL	= $16.00

I use my $25.00 gift card to pay for the diapers, making them free, and I still have $9 in credit left over. What a steal!

> **HOT TIP:** Spend Ten Cents or Less
>
> I always strive for free, but if I have to pay, I won't spend more than ten cents a diaper. That's my personal limit and one you, too, can easily reach if you commit yourself to only buy diapers that are on sale and you have coupons for. If it's a pack of forty, don't pay more than four dollars for the whole package. At that price, you're likely to have enough ECBs, Register Rewards, or CATs to cover the cost and pay nothing out of pocket.　　　　　　　　　　　　　　　　✄

You Asked It

Q: *Besides the SmartSource, RedPlum, and Procter & Gamble Sunday coupon inserts, where else can I find high-value coupons for diapers?*

A: *The following retailers and online destinations tend to have the best, high-value coupons for diapers on a regular basis.*

- *Target*
- *Babies R Us*
- *Rite Aid*
- *eBay*

In addition (and especially for those of you who just can't suspend your brand loyalty), visit your favorite brand website and see what coupons and special deals are available. Often, when you become a member of sites like www.huggieshappybaby.com and www.pampers.com (see the full resource list at the end of the chapter), you're rewarded with freebies and member discounts. Plus membership is usually free.

Wipes

Repeat after me: "I will not spend my hard-earned money on baby wipes any more." I mean, really, what women wants to waste her bucks on *that* part of the mommy job? By combining store markdowns and coupons, wipes almost always work out for free. The real trick with getting wipes for free is to use your high-value coupons on smaller, individual packs, including travel and trial sizes. Be sure to cruise the clearance end caps for baby wipes, diapers, and bottles. *End cap*? This is just coupon-speak for the "end" of the aisle. End caps are reserved for heavily marked down products.

Again, the following shopping strategies are how I tend to score wipes for free. Give each one a try and then decide which strategy works best for you.

Shopping Strategy #1: The CATALINA Deal

> Spend $40, Get $20
> Pampers wipes presale price $7.99
> Pampers sale price $2.99

Purchase five packs for a pre-sale subtotal of $39.95. Throw in a jar of baby food for $0.45 to bring the pre-sale total cost over $40.00 to trigger the $20 back in CATs. Your out-of-pocket cost is only $14.95 (5 x $2.99.) That's a $5 money maker, and all your wipes are FREE.

Shopping Strategy #2: Buy Trial Sizes

Both Walmart and Kmart stores typically carry small packages of HUGGIES wipes for $1.00. With a $1.00-off ANY HUGGIES coupon (and these are easy to come by in the Sunday inserts), the wipes are free. Get your hands on as many of these coupons as you can and stockpile!

HOT TIP: Face the Ugly Truth

Mommies-to-be: While you're stocking up on diapers for your new baby, don't overlook "coverage" for yourself. There's just no delicate way to say this—once that baby comes you're going to need to stuff your drawers with extra-absorbent maxi pads. Trust me, it's not pretty, so start stockpiling them now for free. The same shopping rules apply—combine a coupon with a clearance deal to get them for free. Save yourself a desperate run to the store later on.　　　　　　　　　　　　✂

Shopping Strategy #3: The Target Gift Card

Target regularly offers its customers gift cards for buying participating products. I cashed in on a deal where if you bought two packages of ANY wipes, you got a $5 gift card. I found two small packages that were priced at $3.49 each, totaling $7.00. I used two MFR coupons for $1 off/1 package to bring the total cost down to $5. I paid $5 out of pocket and got a $5 gift card back, making the wipes FREE. I rolled this deal until I had a sizable stockpile to take home.

Shopping Strategy #4: Double Your Money

Look for deals on wipes that allow you to use a doubled high-value coupon. Doubling is key. For example, if HUGGIES wipes are on sale for $1.49 and you have a $0.75-off coupon that doubles, the wipes are no cost to you.

Formula

You will always find high-value formula coupons in the Sunday inserts and—*you guessed it*—on eBay. But the easiest way to score free formula is by registering online with all the big formula companies: Enfamil,

Similac, and Gerber. You can register as soon as you find out you're pregnant. Almost all of them will be happy to send you free samples and coupons for formula throughout your pregnancy and first year. Similac's "StrongMoms" program outfits new mommies with a Similac Sling Pack stuffed with formula samples and coupons before you even leave the hospital. I know women who, in addition to receiving a generous amount of formula after registering online with Similac, Enfamil, and Gerber, received free diaper bags, rattles, sippy cups, pacifiers, articles, and advice, *plus* high-value coupons from partner brands. Mommies, it doesn't get better than this. The next time your baby goes down for a nap, get on the computer and sign up for these fantastic freebies.

Also, every time you visit the pediatrician (which feels like every other day that first year), ask for formula samples. Manufacturers regularly send samples of the latest formula recipes to pediatricians for patients to try. Ask when you're checking in or out. The receptionist usually has a stash behind the counter and will be happy to give some to you. You should also ask your doctor. He or she is likely to have some free samples in the examining room. And if you spend any amount of time in the waiting room, you're likely to find formula coupons in many of the parenting magazines.

Unless you're getting it for nothing, I suggest you prolong stockpiling formula until *after* your baby comes. Your baby may be lactose

---

HOT TIP: Get a Free Potty Training Kit
Pampers offers a free Potty Training Kit, including a free sample of Easy Ups Trainers, high-value coupons, stickers and coloring pages, step-by-step training tips, a Potty Progress Chart, and a training trophy. Sign up at www.pampers.com/en_US/potty-kit-request.   ✂

intolerant, need a special soy formula, or prefer a specific brand. Better to wait and find out what your baby's wants and needs are before dedicating an entire cabinet in your bathroom to the wrong formula. On the other hand, if you stockpile formula that you cannot use, there's sure to be another new mother in the neighborhood who would appreciate the hand-out.

Baby Food

Unless you're making it yourself from the fruits and veggies you're growing on your patio or backyard, the easiest way to score free baby food is by combining a store sale with a manufacturer coupon that doubles. Like with wipes, doubling is key because it will almost always make your baby food free. Be on the lookout for coupons for new products from name brands like Gerber and Beech-Nut. Also, sign up for the e-newsletter on Beechnut.com to receive special offers and join Start Healthy, Stay Healthy, a free online program through Gerber.com for exclusive deals and discounts on baby food.

Every time a new product line is introduced (or sometimes simply a new flavor or a redesign of the packaging), manufacturers issue high-dollar-off coupons, "Try Me for Free" coupons, Buy One, Get One

---

SHOPPER'S
Hall of Fame

"I got many free samples from formula companies. You just have to call their 800-number and ask to join their program. I think my best free baby food story is when I signed up for the Beech-Nut newsletter, referred a friend, and got coupons for a $1 off three jars of food. I was able to get many free jars when they were on clearance for $0.29 each."

Zsana, La Quinta, California

Free, and rebate deals in the Sunday inserts and online. If you start noticing coupons for a new Beech-Nut flavor of baby food, it's likely that a store near you is also doing a promotional push, and the product is on sale. You know what that means—cash in and stock up.

Baby Gear

Around the first of the year, many retail stores like Babies R Us and Target start marking their baby gear way down in an effort to move out the last season's inventory and make room for the new spring line. When I was pregnant with my youngest, I got nearly all my baby gear at Target in February for practically nothing. I scored a super stylish Maclaren baby stroller for 75 percent off. I got a Graco Pack N' Play, regularly $120, on sale for $29.99. I found a high-quality high chair for $14.99 and an Evenflo car seat for $10! These are better than consignment shop prices, and the products are brand new. Mark it on your calendar right now—hit the Target baby aisle in February.

You can almost always find a bargain in the baby gear department in Marshall's, Kohl's, JCP, and T.J. Maxx, but if you ask me, Babies R Us has the most sensational deals and discounts on baby gear from bedding to bath products, toys, and clothes. Sign up for the free "Rewards R Us" program at www.babiesrus.com or in a Babies R Us store, and you'll receive all sorts of promo deals and money-off coupons throughout the year. If you haven't delivered yet, sign up for the baby registry and get even more money-off coupons to use in store or online. I've combined MFR coupons with Babies R Us clearance items many times and gotten products for practically nothing. And Babies R Us holds special free events where they show mommies how to use all their new gear, like a Car Seat Workshop and Breast Pump 101.

I've also had beaucoup success shopping the Freecycle Network at www.freecycle.org. Freecycle is a grassroots, nonprofit group of people who are giving, and getting, stuff for free in their own towns. Their credo is to keep it out of the landfills. If you're into the conservation thing, you might also try Craigslist at www.craigslist.org for big-time savings on baby gear. Generally, it won't be new (although many postings boast "never used"), but since our babies grow out of their gear before it's barely broken-in, you can often score killer deals on nearly new strollers, sleepers, high chairs, and car seats. *Better off safe:* It's always best to reference the latest "Recall" list before bringing used baby gear into your home.

As far as baby clothes go, my son's the best dressed in the family. He's been wearing new clothes from Baby Gap, Gymboree, and The Children's Place since day one. And guess what—I didn't pay one red cent. In Chapter 10: Scoring Clothes for Nada, I explain how you can outfit your kid and yourself in name brands for pennies— literally.

As I've preached all along, fantastic free deals are everywhere. Continue to keep your eyes open and look for ways to work it. Often the best deals are the result of calculative planning and creative thinking. This takes a little extra time and effort, but it pays off.

Free Drugs

Now that your baby's covered, I want to share with you what I've been explaining to enthusiastic older crowds—how to beat the system legally and get medical prescriptions for a fraction of the cost, and often for free. Now you don't have to have an AARP card to benefit from the information I'm about to share, so no jumping ahead. Everyone I talk to, the young and mature, has a similar complaint about the high cost of prescriptions, but not me. I've figured out a way to say goodbye to expensive co-pays and ridiculous drug costs. That's a cross-generational benefit!

Flipping Prescriptions

Pharmacies are in it to win it. Prescription drug sales is a competitive business worth big bucks, so the marketing minds for pharmacies like Rite Aid, CVS, and Walgreens are constantly inventing new ways to steal you and your wallet away from the other guys. One of their more successful strategies has been to offer you, the consumer, cash back for transferring your prescriptions from a competing pharmacy over to theirs. You've probably noticed offers like this at your local pharmacy or grocery stores: *Free $25 Gift Card with New or Transferred Prescription.* Shoppers, this is a huge moneymaking opportunity, and I'm not referring to the profits the pharmacy enjoys for snatching up your business. I'm talking about the mullah you get to stuff in your pocket.

You know me. I'm always lusting after new ways to save a buck, so when I realized that I could not only save my precious dollars, but also multiply them by three and four by "flipping" prescriptions, I did a victory dance in the aisles. My co-pay for most prescriptions is five dollars. So using the example above—*Free $25 Gift Card with New or Transferred Prescription*—for every prescription I transfer, I make a twenty-dollar profit. When I first caught whiff of this deal, I unloaded my bathroom cabinets searching for prescriptions with remaining refills on them. I was actually surprised that I had so many basic prescriptions (iron and fluoride supplements, allergy and asthma meds, for example) with available refills. I took a total of five prescriptions into CVS and asked to transfer them all from my existing pharmacy. "No problem," they said and asked that I return in thirty minutes. Really, it could not have been easier. *Note:* For every prescription you transfer, you must have proof of the prescription (either a written script from your doctor or the bottle itself) and a Transferred Prescription coupon. You can find these coupons in store circulars, ads, and online. Make sure to ask the cashier to ring each order up separately. For example, you might say, "Good afternoon. I'd like to transfer three

---

HOT TIP: Include Your Pets

You can fill your pet's prescriptions at most pharmacies now, which means you can throw your kitty/doggy/bunny's prescription into the mix when transferring scripts to another pharmacy.   ✂

---

prescriptions. I have a coupon for each. Would you please ring them up separately?" And while they're ringing up your separate orders, high-five yourself for making the system work for you.

Checklist
Transferring Prescriptions

✓ Locate Transferred Prescription coupons in your pharmacy circulars, grocery store sale ads, or online. And don't be afraid to ask store employees what freebies they have behind the counter.

✓ Bring your old prescription bottle, or paper prescription from your doctor, into the pharmacy. *Note:* You must transfer your prescription in-store versus online to receive a gift card.

✓ If you haven't filled a prescription in that pharmacy before they will ask you about insurance, any known allergies, etc.

✓ They'll call over to your existing pharmacy and ask them to transfer all your information over.

✓ Pick up your prescription(s) later that day along with your cash-back coupon or gift card.

✓ If you have more than one prescription, make sure the cashier rings them up separately with each Transferred Prescription coupon to get the maximum number of gift cards.

The first time I transferred prescriptions, I made $100 in store gift cards. Woo Hoo! After that win, I was eager to try my luck again. The following month I transferred my prescriptions from CVS to Walgreen's and made another $100.00 there. I did the same thing with Rite Aid the month after that. At the time, all three pharmacies were offering $25 store gift cards for transferred scripts, so with my $5 co-pay, I was up $300 in three months by simply transferring prescriptions from one store to the other. After Rite Aid, my shopping strategy hit a new "flipping" level. I flipped my prescriptions back to Target, which is where I started and where they were offering $10 gift cards with purchase of any new or transferred prescription. A month later, I flipped my prescriptions from Target back to CVS, then back to Walgreens from CVS, and so on and so on. As long as you have prescriptions to refill, you can continue to flip them and let the money add up.

Now before you lose your flippin' mind over this amazing money maker, read the fine print on your Transferred Prescription coupons. Some pharmacies won't consider a prescription "new" or "transferable" until three months have passed since the last time you had a prescription filled there. For example, if I transferred my prescriptions from Target to Walgreens in January and from Walgreens to CVS in

---

HOT TIP: Tap into Their Competitive Spirit

Do you have more than one pharmacy in town? If so, chances are they accept each other's coupons. Your CVS Transferred Prescription coupon will very likely be accepted at Walgreens and vice versa. Of course, ask your pharmacy if they honor competitor coupons before you slap one down on the counter and expect a free gift card.   ✂

February, I'd have to wait until April before I could flip them back to Walgreens. Get it? Although, *(shhhhhh)*, most pharmacies don't enforce the three-month rule and if you live somewhere with several competing pharmacies, by the time you flip back around, three months have probably passed anyway.

As far as I'm concerned, if you don't flip a script every time you have a prescription that needs to be refilled, you're throwing away free money. Now I realize that not everyone has the low prescription co-pay I do. But even if your standard co-pay on prescriptions is twenty bucks, you're likely to still make money by transferring your prescriptions. Or at the very least, break even. And I'm stating the obvious here—when you break even, you're essentially not spending any money. If your co-pay is twenty dollars and you receive a twenty-dollar gift card for transferring your prescription, then your meds are free. Who doesn't love that?

Get with the Program

Not all prescription programs are created equal, so if you're someone who has multiple prescriptions to fill every month, shop around, find the best "flipping" deals and make the system work for you. Below is a list of some of the more popular, national drug store chains. Because stores switch up their programs and promotions with some regularity, confirm your store's transferred prescriptions policy before you get in the pharmacy checkout line.

Walgreens — Walgreens generally offers $25 for every transferred script. That's about as high as transferred prescription coupons go. Look for Wags coupons in the weekly circular and online. If you already fill your prescriptions at Walgreens, they will often reward you with store credit for refilling an existing prescription for the first time online. Check the in-store circular and online for their latest deals and promotions. Also, if you become a Walgreens cardholder, you're

---

SHOPPER'S
Hall of Fame

"My husband and I have on-again/off-again allergies, so I often transfer my scripts to gain gift cards. I once transferred a script from a pharmacy to Genuardis and received a $30 gift card. I picked up a pack of New York strip steaks, Jimmy Dean sausage, and bagels with my earnings. I've also used a transferred prescription coupon for Target at CVS and transferred a script for a $10 gift card. I combined that with a rain check I had for Scott's toilet paper and got thirty-six rolls for $6.49 and still had $3.50 left over."

Stacey, Middleton, Massachusetts

---

invited into the Prescription Savings Club where you'll save on more than 5,000 brand name and generic medications. Generic meds are priced at $12 for a 90-day supply—that's $4 a month. Plus, members get an additional 10% off store brand products. Not bad, but club membership isn't free. Enrollment is $20 per year or $35 for your entire family. And you're not eligible if you're enrolled in a publicly funded health care program, such as Medicare, Medicaid, or the military benefit program, TRICARE.

Kmart — Kmart generally offers a $25 Kmart Gift Card with the purchase of a transferred prescription and $10 for any new script. Find these coupons in the Kmart store flyers. Like Walgreens, Kmart has a Prescription Savings Club where you can buy generic prescription medications for $5 after paying the $10 club membership fee. A 90-day supply is $15. Generic meds are a bit more at Kmart, but the membership fee is much lower than the Walgreens Prescription Savings Club, and it's extended to your entire family. Plus, after you've joined the club, Kmart will give you $10 back in store credit that you can use toward the purchase of prescriptions. Members also receive up to 35 percent off generic prescription medications and up to 20 percent off all other brand-name prescription medications.

Target — Like Kmart, Target rewards its customers with a $10 gift card with purchase of any new or transferred prescription. In addition, Target will fill any generic prescription for $4 for 30 days or $10 for 90 days.

How to really work it: Transfer a prescription to Target and receive your $10 gift card. The following month, if you're willing to try a generic equivalent, use your $10 gift card to get a 90-day supply for free. Or, as soon as you get your $10 gift card for transferring a script, turn right around and use it to fill another order. Also, when you enroll in Target Pharmacy Rewards and fill ten prescriptions using your RED card (Target's store credit card), you'll receive a Target Pharmacy Rewards certificate good for 10 percent off a day of shopping at Target.

HOT TIP: Play Your Cards Right

You cannot pay for your new or transferred script with the gift card you are about to earn. Technically, the gift card isn't yours until you pay for your new or transferred script, the transaction is complete, and you're handed a receipt. So, say you go into your pharmacy with two scripts you want to transfer from another pharmacy. The pharmacy will transfer and fill your first order, charge you the co-pay, and then give you a gift card. You cannot use *that* gift card to pay for your first script. But, you can use your gift card to pay for the second script. Make sense?   ✄

Walmart — Like Target, Walmart also offers $4 generic prescription drugs every day of the week without any fee to join any special program. I told you the pharmacy biz was competitive, didn't I? Look for Walmart Transferred Prescription coupons in the Walmart weekly store ads. If you can't find any current offers, try taking in a competitor's coupon and ask if they'll honor it. If you don't have any competitor coupons, go to eBay (of course) and search for "coupon prescription" or "transferred prescription," and I guarantee you'll find many to choose from.

Rite Aid — When you transfer a prescription at Rite Aid, you'll receive a $25 gift card, plus twenty-five points for every prescription on your wellness+ Rewards Card toward additional savings, including 20 percent off non-prescription purchases.

How to really work it: Before you transfer your prescription to Rite Aid, see if your medicine is on Walmart's or Kmart's list of $4 prescriptions. If it is, print a copy of the list and take it with you to the pharmacy. Rite Aid will more than likely match a competitor's price, which means that you could transfer your prescription to Rite Aid, get the $25 gift card, and only pay $4 out of pocket for your medication. Is that a red-hot deal, or what?

CVS — CVS also offers $25 gift cards for new or transferred prescriptions. How to really work it: Use your $25 gift card to purchase CVS sale items that reward you with Extra Care Bucks. Use your ECBs to pay for future prescriptions.

Find CVS Transferred Prescription coupons in the weekly circular and by scanning your ECB card at the Extra Care coupon center (that's the big red machine toward the front of the store that spits out coupons). Remember: Always scan your card as soon as you enter the store, or you'll forget and miss out on savings just waiting to print!

Dose and Dash

So you thought *those* deals were good. What if I told you some pharmacies are just giving drugs away because they want to help you out? It's true. Many pharmacies and grocery food chains have started giving away free antibiotics. That's right. Select antibiotics and pre-natal vitamins are free in the following stores as long as you have a valid prescription. Of course, any store reserves the right to modify or discontinue an offer at anytime, which is why, again, I say do your homework before hitting the aisles. And just because your local chain isn't listed below doesn't mean it isn't offering a similar deal. Be sure to ask!

- Giant Eagle
- Giant Food
- Meijer
- Publix
- Schnucks
- ShopRite
- Stop & Shop
- Safeway
- Walmart
- Wegmans Food Mart

Before moving on to the next chapter and while they're still fresh in your mind, I want to encourage you to pass on my top-level shopping strategies. In fact, I insist that you do. When I was a young mother, struggling and scared I wouldn't make the rent every month, I could have really benefited from the information in this chapter. So even if you aren't pregnant or a new mom, there's sure to be a girlfriend, co-worker, or woman in your neighborhood who'd be delighted to hear that she no longer has to spend her money on high-priced diapers and wipes. And what about your parents, grandparents, or the nice couple across the street? Are they feeling crippled by the cost of prescription drugs? Show these people the secret to flipping scripts and shopping for free so they can worry less and enjoy life more.

Resources

Diapers
Huggies: www.huggieshappybaby.com
Luvs: www.luvsdiapers.com
Nature Babycare: www.naty.com
Pampers: www.pampers.com
Seventh Generation: www.seventhgeneration.com/diapers

Formula
Enfamil: www.enfamil.com
Gerber Good Start: www.gerber.com
Similac: http://similac.com

Baby Food
Beech-Nut: www.beechnut.com

Free Baby Samples and Discounts
Babies Online: www.babiesonline.com
Babies R Us: www.babiesrus.com
Baby to Bee: www.babytobee.com
Craigslist: www.craigslist.org
Freecycle Network: www.freecycle.org
Freeflys: www.freeflys.com
Pampers Free Potty Training Kit: www.pampers.com/en_US/potty-kit-request

Baby Products
Johnson's Baby: www.johnsonsbaby.com
Playtex Baby: www.playtexbaby.com

Free Antibiotics
Giant Eagle: www.gianteagle.com/pharmacy/free-antibiotics
Giant Food: www.giantfood.com/antibiotics
Meijer: www.meijer.com/pharmacy
Publix: www.publix.com/freeantibiotics
Safeway: www.safeway.com
Schnucks: www.schnucks.com/pharmacyprogram.asp
ShopRite: www.shoprite.com/cnt/pharmacy.html
Stop & Shop: www.stopandshop.com/antibiotics
Walmart: www.walmart.com
Wegmans Food Mart: www.wegmans.com

Drug Stores
CVS: www.cvs.com
Kmart: www.kmart.com
Rite Aid: www.riteaid.com
Target: www.target.com
Walgreens: www.walgreens.com

10

Scoring Clothes for Nada

I don't want to downplay the importance of free medicine to treat an ailment or illness, but scoring free clothes feels *almost* as beneficial to my health, and I don't know many women who, if they're being honest, wouldn't admit to feeling the same way. If you're someone whose mood can go from high bitch to euphoric after encountering a super sale at your favorite clothing store, you're going to love this chapter. I will reveal how I dress my kids in Abercrombie & Fitch, Gap, Nike, North Face, and Old Navy for free. What's more, I share my tricks for snagging clothing for me . . . and for less than a latte.

What's in the cart?

Here's what you'll find in this chapter:
- My killer two-for-one shopping strategy
- How creating your own eBay boutique could change your life (and save you $$$)
- Hot tips for *really* working outlet malls
- The secret to off-season shopping

Playing Doubles

I mentioned in Chapter 9: You're Covered: From Diapers to Drugs, that when I was pregnant with my fourth child, I shopped Target's awesome February sales for baby gear. When I found a deal I couldn't pass up (like an Evenflo car seat for ten bucks—*hello bargain!*), I'd buy two, sell one on eBay to cover my out of pocket costs, and keep one for free. This two-for-one shopping strategy is one I frequently use to score free clothes, and I'm going to walk you through the process step-by-step. Hold on: You didn't think I was going to whisper a secret code to a hidden door in your ear where retail fairies handed you shopping bags of free name-brand clothes, did you? Sorry, girls. Shopping for free clothes isn't that easy. Believe me, I wish it were, but scoring bonus blouses, tops, skirts, dresses, jeans, shoes, and accessories takes creative strategy and work. But, you get that, right? We're talking new clothes. For nothing. Effort is required.

Note: For those of you who aren't into the eBay thing, before you go skipping ahead, hear me out. I think you might change your mind. If not, my feelings won't be hurt. Deal?

Shopping for clothes for free all started when I discovered a superabundance of coupons on eBay. Once I did, I spent many happy hours bidding on high-value coupons that I could combine with store sales. As you now know, too, eBay has coupons available for nearly

---

HOT TIP: Pay It off Immediately

Only use store credit cards if you can promise yourself that you'll pay the balance off every month (or better yet, immediately following your transaction). Shopping for free is great, but not if you have to pour your hard-earned cash back into interest charges and fees.　　　　　　　　　　✂

every store in your local mall and free promo codes are all over the Internet, so it wasn't long before I was making out like a bandita. For example, a J. Crew little black dress marked down to 50 percent off is already a steal, but if you throw a $10-off coupon on top of the deal, and use your store charge card to take another 15 percent off, your savings are huge.

For months, I had fantastic success shopping for clothes using the match coupons + sales method. A lot of the time, my purchases were free. Yet, I couldn't figure out how to consistently hit my zero goal at the register.

That all changed the day my daughter asked me for a new pair of Heely's (these are the kids' sneakers that double as roller skates. Think Dr. Arizona Robbins on *Grey's Anatomy*). I argued that her old Heely's were in decent shape and she didn't need another new pair quite yet. My twelve-year-old daughter, who is a quick study and a budding bargainista herself, suggested I sell her old Heely's on eBay to help pay for new ones. Interesting concept. Where did she get that?

I took the bait and listed her used Heely's on eBay, along with the tool that pops the wheels in and out. As the auction counted down, the bids went higher and higher. I thought, *This kid is onto something. I guess the apple doesn't fall far from the tree.* The highest bid was at nineteen dollars when she announced she'd lost the Heely's tool. *Arghhh!* She's a smart shopper, but she's still a scattered kid. So my husband and I tore off to the local Bob's Store to find a replacement tool before the auction ended. After finding a $10 tool kit, which I was reluctant to pay for, I stumbled upon one of Bob's monster clearance sales. Brand new Heely's still tucked into their shoeboxes were selling for ten bucks a pair—tool included! I thought, if used Heely's are selling for nineteen bucks a pair on eBay and I can buy new Heely's for ten—*Cha Ching*—that's a profit just waiting to happen. I gave my husband "the look," and he dutifully ran off in search of a cart.

We bought nineteen pairs of new Heely's that day. They sold on eBay for an average of $31.50 a pair—a great deal for eBay customers and more than a $20.00 profit, per pair, for me. Needless to say, after that unexpected fortune, I was hooked on Heely's. I was on the phone to Bob's Stores up and down the North Shore in search of every marked down pair in existence.

I worked this deal for as long as I could find Heely's and then I rolled my eBay profits into another hot "get." In my neck of the Northeast, it was DC-brand snowboarding boots. These trendy, high performance kicks are popular with skater kids and snowboarders and they regularly go for $179.00 a pair, but I found them in August selling for $39.99 on the popular designer discount site www.6pm.com (major steal). I bought and resold six pairs on eBay just before the snow season started in November for $89.99, making a $50.00 profit on each. This was a short-lived moneymaker because the new season's hot style arrived shortly on the scene, downgrading my boots to the less desirable pile. And that's what's tricky about reselling on eBay— knowing how to play the popularity game. A lot of the time, it just comes down to dumb luck, but there are a few simple rules by which I've learned to play.

HOT TIP: Start with the Basics

If you're not yet a member of eBay or if you've bought on the auction site but never sold anything, I suggest going to http://pages.ebay.com/education/index.html where you'll be directed to the "Seller Information Center" for everything you need to know about selling on eBay. It's quite a short and simple process, so don't shy away. Before you know it, you'll be up and running, *err*, selling.   ✂

Checklist
Reselling on eBay

✓ Do some research ahead of time. Is your item in demand?
Meaning—is there already a lot of inventory on the site and
is it demanding a high price and moving fairly quickly?
If not, don't bother.

✓ If your item is hot and you're likely to make a profit, buy
multiples and immediately list them on eBay.

✓ List your product at a competitive price (I tend to go a little
lower than the average selling price) and sell it at a "Buy It
Now" fixed amount or as a 24-hour auction item.

✓ Stay in competition by routinely checking how prices are
fluctuating and price adjust.

✓ When prices start to plummet, slash your asking price, offload your items, and get out of the game.

Mall Rats Get the Best Cheese

Once I realized I could purchase multiples of a hot item, resell them
all at a bargain price on eBay (minus the little ditty I'd occasionally
keep for myself), and still make a profit, I went crazy in the clothing
department. I started by stalking sales in all the name-brand mall
stores. It's no secret that nearly every store eventually puts its
merchandise on sale, but you've probably noticed that some store
markdowns are better than others. For example, Banana Republic falls
into the "super sales" category. Banana Republic rotates its inventory
frequently, which means that that periwinkle cashmere sweater you
had your eye on last month but couldn't rationalize paying top dollar
for could easily be hanging on the sales rack next month. (Any shopper
worth her salt knows the sale stuff is in back and often along the
perimeter of the store, but I think it's worth the reminder because

too often we become mesmerized by all the shiny, new merchandise hanging in the front when often the best gems are in the back.)

Get to Know the Routine

Because I'm a mall rat who keeps watch on my favorite stores, I started to take notice when inventory made its way from the front of the store to the back (this varies store to store). Eventually the periwinkle number I'd coveted when it was on window display was banished to the back and marked down to $14.99. I did a double take. Fifteen bucks for quality cashmere—are you kidding me? This was a deal almost too good to be true, so before someone told me otherwise, I bought every discounted cashmere top I could get my hands on. I spent a couple hundred dollars for thirteen sweaters and then listed all but one on eBay. After they sold—and again, they all did because I start the bidding at a generous price—I made all my out-of-pocket expenses back and hung a beautiful new sweater in my closet that, at the end of the day, cost me nothing. What's more, I turned a ridiculous profit and, this, my fellow shoppers, is how to shop for clothes for free.

Now I can't promise this same opportunity will present itself to you, so don't show up on my doorstep demanding your discounted cashmere. But I will go so far as to say—if you're willing to follow my lead and take a similar gamble playing the eBay game—it's likely to pay off.

After my cashmere score, I worked the malls for a while. I eventually got to the point where I knew most of my favorite stores' markdown schedule and their unique discount opportunities. I learned, for example, that at Gymboree, the sweetie-pie apparel store for newborns and kids, when you join the Gymboree member program, you earn $25 for every $50 you spend in the store. A 50 percent savings always catches my eye, and $25 actually goes a long way on children's clothes at Gymboree when you buy off the clearance rack

---

SHOPPER'S
Hall of Fame

"When my daughter was young I wanted to be a stay-at-home mom but still have a little cash in my pocket for myself. I started selling Gymboree clothes that I got for super cheap using Gymboree 'Gymbucks' on clearance deals. I remember once walking out of Gymboree with two huge bags of clothes I paid a total of $125 for after 'bucks' and discounts. After re-selling on eBay, I made over $1,000. My daughter was virtually dressed for free by reselling on eBay, and I had that nice pocket full of cash."

Drueann, Boxford, Massachusetts

---

and slap a dollar-off coupon on top of the deal. I found that for $25, I could dress my youngest like a pampered prince and still have merchandise left over to resell on eBay. I also discovered that, even used, Gymboree garments held their value on eBay, so when he grew out of his princely duds, I resold them on eBay and made back every penny I initially invested.

You Asked It

Q: *How do you know what products are worth buying multiples of and reselling on eBay?*

A: *The key is being able to identify what's hot at the moment. If you don't have a clue, then ask your kids, your babysitter, the student intern at the office, or your trendiest girlfriends. Chances are, they'll know what the "must-haves" of the moment are. It's important to understand the difference between a trend and a solid brand. A trend, like Team Jacob* *t-shirts or Carrie Bradshaw-does-Morocco gladiator sandals, will enjoy a seasonal spike in popularity, and then just as soon as the leaves turn, they'll be replaced on the shelves with the next big thing. A solid brand or product, like a classic Calvin Klein trench or a dependable pair of Levi's, never goes out of style, or demand.*

Checklist
Shopping for Clothes for Free

- ✓ Stalk your favorite stores. How much of a stalker you want to be is up to you, but I become a familiar face in the stores I shop. I suggest dropping by once a week until you learn the stores general retail ebb and flow.
- ✓ Learn the markdown schedule. Each store's schedule will vary, which is why being a loyal customer (i.e., stalker) can work in your favor. When a store I frequent is about to mark items down, a store employee often tips me off ahead of time. Once an item gets a mark-down sticker, you can be sure it's on its fateful march to the clearance racks in the back.
- ✓ Scour the weekly newspaper ads and glossy inserts for percentage or dollar-off coupons and/or search online for printable coupons to apply to the total sale at checkout.
- ✓ Purchase trendy items that are still "hot" that you can sell quickly at a "Buy It Now" price on eBay. Also, shop for classic pieces that never go out of style.
- ✓ Buy multiples.
- ✓ List what you don't want to personally keep in your own closet on eBay.
- ✓ Use keywords in your listing title. Include the brand name and include the word "new." Also check your spelling! Abercrombie sells well. Aberchromie does not. You may

think this is obvious, but I win a lot of auctions on eBay by shopping for misspelled brand names. I'm usually the only person bidding on a "New Ann Tyler Blouse," for example.

✓ Be fair to your customers. Personally, I like to spread the wealth by starting my bids way below the original retail price. I got a great deal—why shouldn't you?

✓ In the same vein, don't overly inflate your prices: not only is it good to share the wealth, but overinflating means that, eventually, you'll lose customers.

Working the Outlets

From the malls, I took my shopping game to the Kittery, Maine, outlets where shoppers can find name-brand and designer labels at a discounted price. (If you're reading this book I bet you're already aware of the bargains to be found at outlets. Well here's the icing on the cupcake.)

Before heading to any outlet mall, do an online search for printable coupons for the stores you plan on tackling. Remember: Always do an online search of the store you plan on shopping in plus "+ printable coupon" or "+ text code" before you set foot in any store. In addition, go directly to the outlet website. What most shoppers don't know is that exclusive coupons for many of the outlet stores can be printed directly from the main outlet site. Some sites even offer coupon books that you can purchase for a nominal fee that promise hundreds of dollars in discounts. Look also for an online outlet "club" that you can join to enjoy even more special offers (most of these are free to join). And finally, become a fan of your favorite outlet on Facebook. You'll find that secret sales and coupons are often leaked to loyal Facebook fans before they've gone totally public. Do all this *before* heading to the mall. More prep work, yes, but it'll pay off.

Now you're ready to shop. With coupons in hand and a game plan in place, hit the outlet mall store clearance racks where items are often marked down to ten bucks or less. Whenever I come across popular "now" styles and classic pieces at rock-bottom prices, I start grabbing. I buy as many as I can afford and apply my percentage or dollar-off coupon to the total sale. I sell what I don't keep on eBay to break even and often times, I make a profit.

You Asked It

Q: *Is buying up all the best clearance items fair to the other shoppers?*

A: *I'm an opportunist, I admit. But it's not like I'm grabbing anything out of anyone's hands. I'm not going to fight another shopper over a clearance rack. If it's you and me shopping the same discount sale, I'm more than happy to share. But if it's just my shopping cart and me alone with a stack of 90 percent-off garments that no one else seems to want, I'm going to take it all. Finders, keepers.*

Probably the best day of my shopping career happened when I was shopping at my daughters' favorite pre-teen store, Justice. It was a few days before the President's Day weekend. A trusted store manager (I make an ally in every store I shop) whispered in my ear that everything—all the winter coats, skirts, sweaters, jackets—would be on sale for $4.99 that Sunday. Needless to say, I almost threw my arms around her. For the next three nights, I could barely sleep. Finally, on Sunday, I hit the store as soon as it opened and guess what? They'd slapped a 50 percent-off sale on top of the $4.99 deal. Now we're talking $2.50 per item. Major deal alert! Plus, I had a handful of *Spend $50, Save $25* coupons on me, bringing each item down to $1.25. It was almost too much for my heart to take.

At the end of that shopping spree, I, along with the help of three employees, hauled over thirty bags of clothing out to my mini van: faux fur and suede coats, corduroy jackets, puffy vests, velvet dresses, a variety of sweaters, a ton of holiday tops, hats, gloves, and flannel pajamas. Looking back, I'm sure I was a road hazard, driving home with limited visibility out my bag-stuffed back window, but I had to do it. I got well over two thousand dollars worth of clothes for less than a hundred bucks.

If you have pre-teen girls, it's an absolute must to sign up for Justice's e-mail alerts and add your daughter to their birthday club and mailing list. When you do, you'll receive high-value coupons on your daughter's b-day, along with special discount coupons throughout the year that you can apply to their phenomenal sales. For every dollar I spend at Justice, my daughter looks like a million bucks. And when she's happy, Mom scores a few points. And believe me—since she became a pre-teen, I'll take them as often as I can get them.

A Little Less Hard Core

Okay, so you're not interested in buying multiples of the same garment and reselling them on eBay. You don't have the time. You're a hard-core shopper, but you have your limits. You simply want to find killer deals on the racks and be done with it. Fair enough.

For shoppers like you, I'll remind you of the first several rules from the Shopping for Clothes for Free Checklist and add one additional suggestion:

- Stalk your favorite stores.
- Learn the markdown schedule.
- Scour the weekly ads for percentage- or dollar-off coupons and/or search online for promo and discount text codes to apply to your total sale at checkout.

- Use your store credit card to take an additional percentage off your bill, bringing your total costs down even lower. Remember: Only use the Plastic Devil if you can promise yourself that you'll pay as you go.

Oftentimes, by simply taking these steps, you'll be shopping for free clothes in no time. In Chapter 5: Like Getting Paid to Shop, I talked about my fondness for shopping at Kohl's and this is exactly the reason why. Get Kohl's $5-off coupons by signing up for email alerts on www.kohls.com. When you apply the $5-off coupon to a clearance item and take an additional 15 percent off for using the Kohl's credit card, you can shop for free at that store on any given day.

JC Penney is another store where shopping for free is a relative cinch. (JCP is no longer your grandmother's department store. If you haven't been there in a while, you may be pleasantly surprised by its new "hipper" inventory.) With a JC Penney $10-off coupon (not as easy to come by as a $5-off coupon from Kohl's, but they're out there. Hint: eBay) combined with a clearance sale price, you're already more than half way to free in many cases. Top that with a 20 percent-off discount for using your JCP card and you're golden. (BTW, at JCP your card discount is taken off *first* giving you a greater overall savings.)

Say you find a pair of $79 skinny jeans on the clearance rack for $13 (not an impossibility, by the way). After you swipe your JCP credit card giving you 20% off, you owe the store $10.40. Then after you use your $10-off coupon your total bill comes to 40 cents. Not free, but pretty darn close. Plus, if every time you shop at JC Penney you complete the online survey printed on your receipt, you get a coupon for 15 percent off your next purchase. Applying one of those babies to the scenario above, your total cost would come to $0.34 for a pair of bootilicious jeans. If that's not an insane deal, I don't know what is.

You Asked It

Q: *Isn't it true that the clothes that end up on the 50, 75, and 90 percent-off clearance racks are the garments with busted zippers and missing buttons, or simply ill fitting, badly designed clothes that no one looks good in? In other words: stuff I wouldn't want to pay money for anyway.*

A: *If something ends up on the clearance rack it's because it wasn't selling at the original asking price, but not necessarily for the reasons you mention. Sure, sometimes a designer totally misses the mark and creates a garment that doesn't sell. And if you only shop in small boutique stores with a limited inventory, a clearance item may be an unwanted item. But more often than not, the clothes hanging on the clearance rack did sell well when they were in the front of the store; the store simply ordered more inventory than it needed. Think of it this way: Most garments on clearance are simply store overstock. Instead of sending unsold pieces back to the manufacturer or to a warehouse where they'll just sit in a box, stores significantly discount prices in hopes of offloading their inventory. After all, selling at a lower price is better than not selling at all.*

HOT TIP: Buy Off-Season for Kids

If you, too, have kids, be sure to check out the unique savings opportunities and clearance markdowns in the following stores. I've scored big time in each one of them by buying off-season.

- Old Navy
- GapKids
- Baby Gap
- The Children's Place
- Gymboree
- Hollister
- Hanna Anderson
- Aerie
- Aeropostale
- Abercrombie Kids
- Justice
- Nike
- The North Face

✂

The Waiting Game

Buying off season is another one of my most cherished shopping strategies. I'm sure you've noticed that with the first hint of spring come the new spring clothing lines. And when summer begins to fade, store mannequins shed their bikinis for fall tweed jackets. But what you might not know is that when a season peaks, stores go into massive mark-down mode. Racks of perfectly beautiful clothes, now considered "off season" are ushered to the back

---

HOT TIP: Stay Ahead of the Game

I'm a mother of four, who worries that if I don't stay ahead of the game, I'll actually have to pay full price for kids' clothes—yikes, scary thought—so not only do I buy off-season, I buy clothes in advance for my kids. You name it—jeans, sweatshirts, jackets, and shoes—if I find a great deal, I'll buy the next size up for each of them. For example, I can get amazing deals on snow gear in March: winter coats under two dollars, sweaters and snow pants for fifty cents, and sneakers for three bucks. I anticipate what size each of my kids will be wearing the following year, and I stock up. I have a corner in the attic where I stash their clothes for the next season. Big names like Abercrombie & Fitch, North Face, Nike, and Ugg don't go out of style, so I buy what my kids will wear, plus a few extra to resell on eBay and break even. One year I took an entire display of hooded, fleece-lined sweatshirts regularly priced at $29.99, on sale for $1.49 each and resold them all for $17.99. I took the profits and splurged on a Play Station 3 that my kids were begging me for. I paid almost top-dollar for it. Sometimes even I have to break my own rules. ✂

walls where they will wait for you to buy them for a fraction of their original price.

You can get some of the most amazing, jaw-dropping deals by buying off season and timing it just right, and in the next chapter, The Baddest @ss Deals Month by Month, I outline when and where to shop off season throughout the calendar year. As a general rule, start stalking your favorite stores at the peak of the season. *Sneak Peak:* Summer = July, Fall = September, Winter = February, Spring = May. This is when prices start to dramatically drop and you can get some seriously great deals. For example, you can often score on summer sundresses in July. This never makes a whole lot of sense to me because, *well*, it's still summer. It could be one hundred degrees outside, and the only clothes you see women wearing on the street are light, breezy sundresses, yet inside the air-conditioned malls, stores start acting like everyone's planning Thanksgiving dinner.

WORK IT: SHOP LIKE YOU MEAN IT

Before we move on to the next chapter, I want you to focus your shopping strategy on three apparel stores you love and do the following:

- Sign up for the store's e-mail alerts
- Sign up for mobile alerts and coupons
- Join their rewards program
- Enroll in their birthday club
- Become a fan of the store on Facebook
- Take advantage of any store surveys
- Search online for printable coupons and/or promo codes
- Scan the newspaper ads and inserts for high-value coupons

Once you've taken all these steps, put on some comfortable running shoes and, with savings stash in hand, go shop like you mean it! ✂

11

The Baddest @ss Deals
Month by Month

So now you know the basic rules of shopping off season. You can get a great deal on a sassy sundress in July, for example, but did you know that there are less obvious "gets" all year round, like every single month? I'm always one step, one month, or one season ahead, and, after reading this chapter, you will be, too, because I'll teach you how to stay ahead of the shopping game.

Throughout the year, key items drop to bottom-dollar prices, and you're just cheating yourself if you don't take full advantage of these opportunities. So, let's go through every month of the year, and I'll show you what you can get for free, or nearly for nada.

What's in the cart?

Here's what you'll find in this chapter:
- Free pillows, perfume, and bedding in January
- A free winter wardrobe in early March
- A year's worth of free gourmet hot dogs in May
- Office supplies for chump change throughout the summer

- Trendy (think dorm room) gets for nothing in October

Note: There is no way to provide you with a complete list of bad @ss deals because *new* deals are popping up all the time, but what I outline below are sales you absolutely don't want to miss. You can always check www.howtoshopforfree.net for the latest and greatest deals du jour.

January: The Gift That Keeps on Giving

I know this is going to sound like verbal product placement, but Target really is my favorite large retail store. It's so cheap and their stuff is just hip enough—it's the perfect combo for girls who love to shop for free. Seriously, if Target added a martini bar and day care, I would be there Monday through Friday, 9–5. I have yet to find another store that has the killer markdowns that Target has. For some reason, Target only lets items sit out on the floor for so long and then they super-slash prices. For the past two years, I've bought Dyson vacuums (the sexiest machine to clean your carpet) in January for an absurdly low price and then resold them on eBay for a profit. I've also been known to nab Black & Decker power tools, George Foreman grills, KitchenAid mixers, digital cameras, and big screen TVs at 75 percent off in January. The funny thing is that the same make and model will appear back on the floor weeks later at its original retail price. I'm not sure why they do this, but, hey, I don't judge, I just take their deals.

Big markdowns on smaller items are found throughout stores on end caps, the shelves at the end of each aisle. Remember: This is where all the cheap stuff ends up. When I enter a store like Target, I circle the store's outer edges first, taking note of the best savings. If I see an item on sale for 50 percent off, I can be fairly certain that in a few days, or a week, it will drop to 75 percent and if anything is left, 90 percent after that. It's hard to resist jumping at a 50 percent-off sale for something you want or need, but wait. Be patient. It's going to go lower. Just hold your water and watch.

In January, I stock up on anything and everything holiday-related. I know this is tough to do because, enough already. I just finished shopping for Santa. Don't make me go back! The last thing you want to do is buy wrapping paper in bulk. I get it, but you need to toughen up and do it. I'm sure you've noticed January discounts on gift tags and bags, scissors, tape, artificial trees, wreaths, garland, holiday decorations, lights, candles, and holiday dishes, but what you might not know is that if you wait just long enough, it's a get-it-free fest. I stockpile next years holiday loot at 75 to 90 percent off. Additionally, anything that's packaged in the spirit of the season, even dishwashing detergent with snowflakes on the box, will be marked down, down, down. And if you have a coupon to throw on top of that, it's sure to be free.

That wrapping paper goes on sale is kind of a no-brainer, so I want you to think about all the stuff you *thought* you were going to buy before the holidays (like the Dyson for that houseful of guests). Over the Martin Luther King Jr. Day (MLK) weekend, you'll find winter clearances on items that are usually pricey, like throw pillows, bedding, sheets, and dishes. Why? These, too, were popular holiday gifts, so the stores overstocked them and whatever hasn't sold by mid-January, they figure it won't. You can get these items for nearly free because the stores want to move the merchandise out. Old Navy and other mall stores have fabulous 75 percent-off winter wear markdowns over the MLK weekend, too. Flannel pajamas, hats, scarves, and mittens go for almost nothing. Perfume and cologne go on sale in January, so now's the time to stock up on your favorite scents. (Again, anything in holiday packaging and many of the boxed sets will be on clearance at 50 to 75 percent off.) For scented sprays and lotions, hit stores like

> **HOT TIP:** Wait. It'll Drop Lower
>
> When you start to see items drop to 30 to 50 percent off, search the coupon database on www.howtoshopforfree.net. Get your coupons ready, and, when holiday merchandise drops to 75 to 90 percent off, jump on the deal. You should not be paying more than a dime (yes, literally ten cents) for wrapping paper.   ✁

Victoria's Secret and Bath & Body Works. Then cruise CVS and World Market for chocolate samplers and gourmet candy. You're probably thinking, perfume and chocolate are two things I don't need in January. You might not, but what about your sweetheart? Or your kid's teacher? Girls, the second week of January is the perfect time to do your Valentine's Day shopping. Trust me, it'll be here before you know it and then you'll be scrambling, so get it done now on the cheap.

February: Sweet Deals

Cold-weather clothes are super slashed throughout February, March, and April. I often say, "Winter clearance lasts as long as a New England winter. It goes on forever." Expensive snow boots and winter coats go for practically nothing at the first hint of spring. If you start building your winter wardrobe in February, when the first snow storm hits the following year, you'll be ready to drop, roll, and make a snow angel in the front yard.

Last year I bought North Face boots and Denali jackets at REI for crazy low prices. The boots I took home for myself were regularly $120, and I got them for under $30. Not free, but a d*mn good deal. Winter clothes and coats often drop to 75 to 90 percent off in

February. Start stalking Nordstrom's at the beginning of the month for that new pair of boots and wait for the prices to drop. They most surely will and you can save hundreds.

Very much like the day after Christmas, the day after Valentine's Day is when you start seeing markdowns on anything and everything love and romance related. Valentine's Day merchandise will eventually go as low as 90 percent off, so do as I do and buy up those leftover packages of Valentine's Day cards for your kids to exchange next year. (It depends on the store, but the typical schedule for holiday markdowns is 50 percent the day after the holiday, 75 percent off four days later, and 90 percent off the seventh day after the holiday.) I usually pay ten cents a box, and then when the holiday rolls around next year, I'm not frantically running out the night before the school party with a distressed child worried she's going to miss out on all the fun.

Here's another idea. If you're planning a wedding within the year, think about scooping up marriage-themed loot for shower decorations, wedding invitations, and centerpieces.

The President's Day weekend mid-February is a fabulous time to find the clearances in the mall stores I've been talking about. You will find that winter clothes, now considered "off-season," have been reduced to unimaginable prices, and, on top of that, many stores have added an additional 50 percent off the lowest marked price to sweeten the deal.

And finally, if you're newly pregnant, remember that February is the perfect time to waddle into Target. Many retail stores like Target start offloading baby clothing and products in February.

March: Frozen Food Month

March is frozen food month, so clip or print every frozen food coupon you come across and combine them with big sales to get lots for free. Additionally, many grocery retailers promote frozen food month by selling freezers for cheap. If you don't yet have a deep freezer, March is the month to buy one and jam it full. A local chain on the North Shore stuffs their sale freezers with high-value coupons. I know women who have bought two freezers just for the coupons.

In addition to frozen foods, March is the absolute best month to hit the outlet malls. Spring is on its way and so are the new Spring lines; whatever winter clothes are still hanging around need to go. In March, you can often find the kind of coat sales that'll make your fleece-vest wearing girlfriends squirm with envy. It's not terribly inspiring to shop for heavy, fur-lined garments when winter's on its way out, but if you can motivate yourself to do it, you'll be handsomely rewarded for it.

In March, I love to shop at the following outlet stores:

- Calvin Klein
- Ralph Lauren
- Tommy Hilfiger
- Nine West
- Gap and Baby Gap
- Justice
- The Children's Place
- Aeropostale
- Brookstone
- Eddie Bauer
- Crate and Barrel
- Pottery Barn
- and let's not forget Saks Off 5th and Nordstrom Rack!

April: Did You Say, Free?

With April comes Easter, and after all the eggs are dyed and the baskets are found—you guessed it—stores will have free Peeps a plenty. Anything with a bunny or a yellow chicky goes straight onto the clearance rack after the Easter holiday. And I know I run the risk of sounding like a nag, but I have to say it again: When you buy holi-day items after the holiday, you spend pennies and save yourself a hassle down the road. So, buy a few baskets and then move on to your local nursery. Easter lilies that demanded top price before Sunday are marked down at many nurseries by 90 percent. Tulip and daffodil bouquets in your local market also go on sale after the holiday. They're still beautiful, smell wonderful, but they're half the price.

In addition to Easter markdowns, April is the month to cash in on Tax Day breaks. Seriously, after filing a pile of paperwork with the IRS, you could use one, right? Many of your local merchants, along with national chains, recognize that you might need a lift on April 15th and will offer freebies to get you through the day. I've enjoyed free coffee from Starbucks, a free massage from a mall spa, and discounted meals at high-end restaurants. Google "tax day freebies" for a list of what merchants are giving away in your area. And while you're at it, do a search for "Earth Day freebies." You're bound to discover many eco-friendly "gets" available to you for free on April 22nd.

Throughout April, winter clothes will be beyond super-slashed. I already mentioned the killer deals on winter wear in February and March, and by April, if anything's left on the racks, they're practically giving it away. So don't be an April fool—cash in on these deals! Last year in April I found a gold mine in the back of Abercrombie & Fitch and Hollister. For those of you who aren't familiar with these stores, they're designed for the young and trendy who love extremely loud music. Just know walking into that place you're likely to feel tired and old and that you may, in fact, go deaf. Despite this, I love to shop in both stores, particularly for the awesome deals they hide away in the very dark, nightclub-looking back corner of the store. Be forewarned: You may have to hold the price tags right up to your eyes to make out the numbers, but you'll be glad you did. I've found corduroy pants, sweaters, and shirtdresses for $6.99 to $9.99.

May: Stock Up and Cook Out

In May, summer is in the air, most noticeably in the hot dog section of your local grocery store. This is the month to stock up for weenie roasts the rest of the year: Coupons for Bar-S, Ballpark, Butterball, and Oscar Mayer hot dogs are everywhere in May, and, when you combine them with a store sale, they're usually free. Last year, I filled my freezer full of about 280 packages—we cook out a lot! Kraft Food also does a big push in May. You can often get iced tea, lemonade, and salad dressings for free by combining coupons with store promotions. Mustard, ketchup, and relish are usually marked down to $1 a piece and with a 50-cent coupon that you double, you end up paying nothing. Buns are usually on sale but not free. I can generally find good deals, like two packages for a buck and I stock up. In most cases, I have CATs that I can use to pay for them.

Because a girl can only eat so many franks, I'm always happy to find deals for other types of dishes. Before and right after the Cinco de Mayo holiday on May 5th, store sales on taco shells, refried beans, taco seasoning, salsa, and Tabasco allow you to satisfy your craving for Mexican food all year round. Plus, combined with Old El Paso and Ortega manufacturer coupons, you're likely to get it all for free.

In addition to all the free food you'll get in May, you can find substantial markdowns on spring clothes, but your time is limited. Hold up—wasn't I just talking about clearance deals on *winter* clothes last month? Yes, I was. The last of the winter merchandise moves out in April and is replaced by the new spring lines. By late May, spring frocks are on their way out. Like the season, spring inventory doesn't last long. Toward the end of the month, prices on spring garments are probably as low as they're going to go, so if you find something you love at 50 or 60 percent off, grab it before it's gone. This is the one shopping season where I don't suggest holding out for 75 or 90 percent markdowns.

HOT TIP: Birthday Freebies

Don't forget to ask for your birthday freebies. The opportunities to celebrate on the cheap are endless. However you plan
to spend your big day, find out ahead of time what birthday
benefits you have coming your way. Starbucks and Dunkin'
Donuts, for example, will happily get you revved up for free.
Museums and cinemas often offer birthday specials. Spas and
cosmetic retailers are known to offer pampering discounts and
product freebies on your birthday. And if you dine out on your
b-day, be sure to ask your waiter if a cocktail, appetizer, or
dessert is on the house. It usually is. You just have to ask. ✂

June and July: With Butter on Top

Remember back in Chapter 8: Eat Healthy on the Super Cheap,
I told you that my husband and I planted fruit trees and a summer
garden so that we could pick for free? I was able to buy my fruit trees
for dirt cheap in June just before the planting season ends. By mid-
July, it's simply too hot to plant trees, so nurseries try to offload their
inventory. At 75 percent off, cherry trees were going for $3.49 and
varietals of apple were under ten bucks. Plus, I also scored a total of
eight Japanese Maple, Weeping Willow, and ornamental trees for ten
bucks a piece—regularly $99.99. As soon as I get them home, I give
them a good soak and then plant them right away. Of course, your
climate and growing season may vary from mine, but generally start
checking your local nurseries in late May and June for discounts and
when prices plummet, make your move. Also, if you love roses, start
scoping out deals right after Mother's Day. You can usually pick
up beautiful rose bushes a week or two after M-Day for 50 to
75 percent off.

In addition to outfitting your garden in June, this is the month to stockpile popcorn and popsicles, probably not a dietary main stay for most single gals, but if you have kids, having popcorn and popsicles on hand is a quick and easy way to satisfy a pestering child. Last summer, I got over forty boxes of fudgesicles for free at Walmart when I found them on sale for $1 a box and matched them with $1-off coupons.

Here's how I worked the popcorn deal:

Spend $25, Get $10 Back Catalina Deal

Orville Redenbacher's Gourmet Popping Corn pre-sale price was $2.79, so I bought nine for $25.11. The sale price was listed at $1.66, so:

Popcorn presale price $2.79 x 9	= $25.11
Popcorn sale price $1.66 x 9	= $14.94

Remember, the secret to Catalina deals is that you're paying the sale prices, but the pre-sale price is what's counted toward the Spend $25, Get $10 Back deal. At this point, I'd only spent $14.94. Then, I used nine $1-off coupons, bringing my total cost down to $5.94

Popcorn $1.66 sale price x 9	= $14.94
MFR coupons $1 off x 9	− $9.00
WHAT I OWE	= $5.94

Then, I got $10 back, making the entire order free and profiting $4.06. I rolled this deal several times. My kids had free popcorn for the rest of the year, and I splurged on beer and steak tips for my husband with my bundle of store cash.

By late July, prices on all summer clothing, bathing suits, and accessories are slashed to make room for the new fall lines. Stock up on shorts, tanks, tops, dresses, sandals, and flip-flops for next year. Also, don't pass up the huge Target toy clearance in July. Massive markdowns up to 75% on Playskool, Thomas the Tank Engine, Elmo, Fisher-Price, and Milton Bradley toys mean you can make a significant dent in your holiday shopping and spend next to nothing. Yes, I realize it's only July, but if scooping up a few deals now means avoiding holiday hysteria in December, isn't it worth it? *Note:* This sale brings out the most skilled DCH's. They will clear entire shelves and grab toys out of your cart if you don't watch it, so move fast and stay alert.

August: A Penny a Day

In August, Staples has their famed Penny Sale. Here's how it works: Throughout the month, Staples marks down five or six different items each week—things like packs of pencils, pencil sharpeners, folders, erasers, and filler paper—to a penny each. You must spend $5 to get the penny items, but there's an easy workaround. I'll find something with a rebate attached, like copy paper for $4.99, get $4.99 back after rebate, and then all I'm really "paying" for are my penny items. My daughter loves the penny sale because we've turned it into a month-long event. I take my two pre-teen kids along with me and give them each a quarter and let them go for it. They get five or six items, pay for them with their quarter, and still get change back. At the end of the shopping trip, the three of us have picked up a massive amount of office supplies, and we've literally spent pennies. We do this frequently throughout the month, and, by the end of the promotion, we've stock-piled bags and bags of school supplies. Then we take all our loot down to the Community Giving Tree, a program to help and provide relief for underprivileged kids living in high-poverty areas, and we donate it all. It's like Christmas in August, and my daughter looks forward to it all year long.

August isn't just for school and office supplies; you can find super low prices—often up to 90 percent off—on patio furniture, barbeque grills, lawn and flower care, pool chemicals, pool toys, and bug spray. Get a jump on all your outdoor needs for *next* season when stores are basically begging you to haul their summer merchandise off the lot.

September: Wall to Wall Sales

Come September, summer vacation has come to an end (sniff); the kids are back in school (yay!); and the rest of us are back to work. Fall apparel, especially back-to-school duds for kids, starts dropping in price the day after school starts, so don't spend your entire fall clothing allowance in August. You'll be wasting your money! If your kids are like mine, chances are they won't even wear most of their new loot before it goes on sale anyway. Wait and watch the prices drop. In September, lightweight jackets, sweaters, long sleeve shirts, and jeans are available for a fraction of their original cost. By the Columbus Day weekend in October and certainly by Halloween, whatever remains of the season is hanging in the back of the store.

If you didn't get everything you needed at the Staples Penny Sale in August, then September is the time to get your office supplies for free, or nearly free. I usually get two cases of printer paper for nothing when I combine coupons with a Staples, OfficeMax, Office Depot, or Target store promotion. Packages of loose-leaf paper will be as low as 9 cents a package at Target. Coupons for $1 off combined with a store sale or clearance will allow you to get high-quality pens and Post-it Notes for free. I can't tell you how many packages of Post-it Notes we've gotten for free—enough for my kids to blanket four walls with "Post-it Note wallpaper" on a rainy day. *Note:* Keep your stash of Post-it Notes away from the children!

October: Cool Deals

If you have a kid in college, October is the best month to snag dorm room "gets." Many stores include dorm supplies in their Back-to-School push and by October, they're ready to move it all out. This is when you can get XL twin sheets (which are very hard to find any other time of year), bedding, trendy plastic dish wear, hanging beads, and other accessories for super low prices. If your college freshman is embarrassed by your attempts to decorate her dorm room, then pass it all off to your pre-teen, who will more than likely consider it cool.

Temperatures are finally starting to drop in October, and most grocery stores take this as their cue to put comfort foods, like soup, broth, and stock on sale. Last year, I got over 200 cans of soup for free by combining store savings with manufacturer coupons. What my family didn't eat, I donated to a local soup kitchen. MMM MMM GOOD.

November: Black Friday

Black Friday (B-F), the day after Thanksgiving, is my absolute favorite day of the year. It's like a religious holiday for those of us who shop for free. The craziest deals, and often the most wacked-out shoppers, can be found tearing through the malls on Black Friday. In my house, for the weeks leading up to B-F, you can feel excitement in the air and find me online casing out the stores I plan to attack. My husband knows that he's on all-day kid duty on B-F. He's heard me threaten more than a few times, "If you work on Black Friday, I will kill you." I need to ride solo in order to stay hyper-focused to get the biggest bang for my buck. Plus, it's really the only day of the year I have totally to myself, so I feel entitled.

On B-F, I leave the house at 5 a.m. dressed in work out gear. I have a thermos of coffee, a few water bottles, and some snacks to last me throughout the day. Once I'm in the car, I start driving out of town.

Contrary to tradition, one of the secrets to B-F is to avoid the malls. I drive out of the way to fringe stores, or to isolated stores with nothing else around them. This way, I get front row parking, and the shelves and clothing racks are full. What you spend in drive time, you will make up for in shorter lines. No crowds. No waiting. Can life get any better than this?

You can use coupons in many stores on Black Friday, so if you have any good ones, take them along, but my advice to you is not to spend too much of your brain power or valuable energy trying to match coupons with sales. I know I'm sounding sacrilegious, but this may be the day to leave the coupons at home. It's chaos already, and fiddling around with your coupon stash is only going to slow you down. On B-F, you want to hit stores like a tornado, scooping up the hippest, hottest items as you move from one department to the next.

Some stores will price match on Black Friday. Find out ahead of time, which do. Hit these stores with any competitor's ad and they will honor the competitive sale price.

Not into crowds as much as you are into deals? No problem. I'm going to let you in on a little secret. You don't actually have to shop Black Friday to get Black-Friday deals. The ads for B-F are often "leaked" about two to three weeks ahead of time and circulated on the Internet. (How and by whom are they leaked? I have no idea. I just say a silent prayer of gratitude.) To cash in on B-F deals in advance, follow this checklist.

Checklist
Advance Planning for Black Friday

- ✓ About three weeks before B-F, do an online search for Black Friday deals. Try searching "Black Friday + sneak peak."
- ✓ Make a list of the items you want to snag and the stores they're in.

✓ Check the store's policy to see if it offers "price protection."
If an item is price protected, then if it goes on sale after
you've bought it, the store will reimburse you the difference.

✓ If your store offers price protection, be sure the store policy
doesn't exclude Black Friday discounts and sales. Read the
fine print.

✓ If B-F sales are included in your store's price protection
policy, buy the items you want ahead of time at their pre-sale
prices. No lines. No waiting. No sold-out merchandise.

✓ On Black Friday, take your receipt into the store with a copy
of the sale ad and get reimbursed the difference on the sale.

✓ If the store with the item you covet *doesn't* offer price protection, find out if your credit card does. Most of the big credit
cards offer price protection.

✓ Charge your item(s) to your credit card before Black Friday
and then on B-F, make a call to your credit card company for
reimbursement.

If, after trying the price protection shopping-strategy on B-F,
you want to give it a go at other times of the year, consider signing up
at www.priceprotectr.com. This online service does all the work of
watching prices for you by tracking the prices of items on your wish
list and/or items that you've already bought and alerting you when
prices drop.

December: The Month to Work It

There's so much free stuff to be had in December even I can't get
it all. In simple terms, December is the month to really work it. In
December, I skip the grocery stores (because I already have everything
I need after loading up like a pro) and spend my shopping hours in
the mall.

All of the large retail stores are competing against each other for holiday shoppers, so they offer insane money-off coupons in December. The values are much higher than what you see at other times of the year, so be on the look out. I will even start a Thursday–Sunday subscription of the *Boston Globe* during that time just so I'm sure to get all the ads. Often, I can get my subscription for free because the *Globe* will run a free trial period during November and December.

One of my favorite December deals is *Buy Any Item and get a $15 item for free.* I always find small things, like nail files, on sale for a buck and, *cha ching,* I've just scored a $15 gift that I can keep for myself or put in someone's stocking. Or here's another good one that I see all the time: *Get $10 off any $10 purchase.* Again, who's doing the math here? With so much on sale in December, and often at prices like five and ten bucks, a coupon like that is your ticket to free stuff compliments of the house.

If you're someone who likes to do the majority of your Christmas shopping online, remember to scour the web for online promo and coupon codes before you hit "Purchase," and visit www.freeshippingday.com for a complete list of the hundreds of popular retailers who offer free shipping on a specified day in December. In 2010, it was December 17th.

Every weekend leading up to Christmas is an opportunity for you to score in a major way if you're religious about combing through the weekly and Sunday newspapers for what will be an over-abundance of high-value coupons. When items are already on sale, and you have a 20 or 30 percent-off store coupon that you either printed or clipped from the paper, and you hit the store when they're taking another 25 percent off, you will get some ridiculous deals. I found a Farberware cooking set this way. The original price was $169.99, and it was marked down on clearance to $17.99. *Oh, Auntie Em, deals like this make me know that I'm home.* I was already giddy after finding this massive markdown, and I had a $10-off any purchase coupon, so now the whole set was costing me $7.99, and then, because I used my credit card, they took an additional 15 percent off. So, I got a 12-piece cookware set for $6.79. Do I hear you cheering for me?

December tends to be a month where people spend more than they want to, but I'm telling you—it doesn't have to be that way. If you work it right, you will get the kind of deals that make you feel like you've done something naughty, and the best part is that you haven't done a single thing wrong, unethical, or un-American. You've played by the rules and gotten more of what you want, but for less.

We've come full circle. Now we're back to the day after Christmas and what goes on sale? That's right! Everything holiday related and this time you'll know just what to do, won't you?

12

Pay It Forward

I've made the point that I'm not a hoarder, yet I've spent the past eleven chapters explaining to you how to stockpile everything from baby wipes to Easter baskets, lipstick to cashmere sweaters. I've even gone so far as to suggest you stash a year's worth of mouthwash under your bed if you live in a small studio apartment. Given that, I wouldn't be terribly surprised if at times throughout this book you found yourself thinking, *This woman is beyond excessive. She amasses more stuff than she could ever possibly use.* That's a fair criticism, and, in fact, you're right on the money. I do load my shopping cart with more than I need, which is why I give so much of it away. Why do I take it in the first place if I don't need it? The answer is very simple: Someone else does.

What's in the cart? ----------------------------------

Here's what you'll find in this chapter:

- My pay-it–forward philosophy
- When to say, *Enough is enough*
- The importance of giving it away

Don't get me wrong. Shopping is my passion, and finding free deals makes me tingle all over. But when it comes right down to it, for me the most rewarding aspect of shopping for free is being able to pay it forward.

Not long after I learned how to shop strategically by matching coupons with sales to get items for free, my stockpile outgrew my family's needs. (Hiring a contractor to build me a 3 by 8-foot pantry for all my overflow loot was the obvious clue.) At that point, I could have taken a chill-pill and scaled back what I threw into my cart each week. But instead, I decided to *grow* my stockpile so I could give to those who don't have the tools to shop like I do and who could use a hand.

The first place I reached out to was the Community Giving Tree, a local program to help and provide relief for underprivileged kids living in high-poverty areas. At the time, the program was asking the community for back-to-school supplies. The woman I spoke to on the phone told me how my donation could help kids like Gabriel, a young boy in a nearby community whose mother couldn't afford simple things like a school backpack for her son. A teacher at Gabriel's school had observed kids teasing him for carrying his books to school in a plastic bag, so the principal contacted the Giving Tree. Through donations, they were able to get a brand-new backpack for Gabriel. The woman on the phone explained how grateful this young boy was to receive this simple gift.

This is the story that inspired me to donate the majority of my free "gets" from the Staples Penny Sale to this organization. Every August, after my kids and I have worked the month-long sale, we drop off bags of pencils, erasers, paper, folders, and markers for kids like Gabriel. I believe this practice has taught my kids to appreciate what they have and value the importance of sharing.

I'm always looking for individuals and organizations that can benefit from my shopping savvy and abundant stockpile. Over the

SHOPPER'S
Hall of Fame

"My brightest 'pay-it-forward' moment was the day I went to the supermarket to load up on free paper towels and toilet paper. I noticed an elderly gentleman dressed in torn and tattered clothing in a motorized shopping cart. I walked up to him and put a half dozen products in his cart and handed him the coupons that would make those products free."

Lannie, Manchester, New Hampshire

"I got word about an elderly couple in town who was struggling to put food on their table. I went through my stockpile and packed up one of everything I had. Then I went to the grocery store, and, for less than ten dollars after coupons, I was able to get them enough fresh produce, meat, juice, and milk to last them two weeks. When I arrived at their house and opened up the back of my Pathfinder and it was overflowing with food, they both just stood there and cried."

Cardinal, Wells, Maine

years, my primary focus has become elderly citizens who simply can't physically do what I do. Remember: Shopping for free is a competitive sport. I donate regularly to the Council on Aging, Meals on Wheels, and various senior centers on the North Shore. I provide toiletries like shampoo, toothbrushes, toothpaste, deodorant, and disposable razors that are super easy for me to get for free but very difficult for someone who is housebound, or simply has a hard time getting around, to shop for and cart home.

As it probably is in your community, too, the list of those in need is endless—senior citizens, veterans, the homeless, jobless, and ailing. Yet often, those in need of our support are the less obvious candidates.

HOT TIP: Take the Path of Least Resistance

I've found that most people won't ask for help even when they desperately need it. I know that when I was a single mom struggling to pay the bills, I never asked to be rescued. I was too proud. I remember thinking, *I don't want to be treated like a charity case.* So when I come across someone who is clearly in a bind but seems reluctant to ask for or receive a handout, I make it easy on them. I give without invitation. Also, I don't take no for an answer.　　　　✂

This past year for example, I reached out to my friend Jane, a mother of three, who was doing very well financially until the economy buckled and she lost her job. And not long after that, her husband lost his and walked out on the marriage. A triple-whammy. Suddenly she found herself fighting to pay a mortgage on an "upside-down" house and still provide a stable environment for her kids (let alone, maintain her own sanity). Jane didn't ask me for help, but I knew she was suffering. One day I called her and said, "Jane, I've done it again. I've brought home more groceries than I know what to do with. I can't find my counter-tops, and my pantry is a mess. Would you mind taking some of if off my hands?" At first she resisted my trying-not-to-be-overt handout, but finally she agreed to let me bring a few things over. I think she was expecting a grocery bag. I showed up with a full trunk of goodies.

Enough Is Enough

After you've been shopping for free for a while, a day will come when you realize you have plenty. You'll look in your pantry or bathroom cabinet and say to yourself, *I really don't need any more*

Special K or Old Spice body wash. When this happens, congratulate yourself. You've reached shopping for free pro status. You have everything you need and then some. Once you let this sense of comfort and safety sink in, I encourage you to take a look around. Think of your extended family, your friends, neighbors, and co-workers. Think of your community. Who do you know who could use a little help?

The Power of Generosity

On October 25, 2009, my community lost Michael Doherty Jr., a beloved kid and my neighbor's teenage son. Michael was killed when the car he was in sped out of control, flipped, and crashed into

---

SHOPPER'S
Hall of Fame

"My sister-in-law recently came into really hard times. I made her a care package of toilet paper, paper towels, deodorant, shampoos, and cleaning supplies. She was so appreciative. I explained to her that these were things I'd gotten for free and she should call for refills anytime. Helping her made my day."

Ashley, Shreveport, Louisiana

"I stocked up on supplies from OfficeMax, Office Depot, and Staples when the stores were practically giving stuff away and shared supplies and shopping tips with a co-worker who was struggling. She learned how to stockpile school supplies for her children, and they blossomed in school and were even put in the gifted program. I feel very happy to have been a positive part of their lives."

Debra, San Francisco, California

---

a cluster of trees not more than 200 yards from his own driveway. My husband and I were the first witnesses on the scene. He died in front of our house.

My husband and I knew Michael well, so his death was both personally shocking and heart breaking. I remember standing outside in the dark after the police cars and an ambulance arrived when I saw Lisa, Michael's mother, running toward her son's body. It was at that moment that I determined to put my personal emotions aside and be strong for her.

Lisa was devastated, as anyone would be. For months she couldn't sleep. She lost her appetite and didn't want to leave the house. She was depressed, and so I reached out the best way I knew how. I emptied my pantry of what my family didn't need and gave it all to her. If she needed something from the store, I'd find a coupon for it and get it for free. When her son's friends held vigils outside the house, I gave the kids my free stockpile of Kleenex, candles, bottled water, and snacks.

I may be guilty of throwing more items into my cart than I personally need, but a tragedy like this is a perfect example of why I shop the way I do. It enables me to help others. It gives me purpose. In the days and weeks following Michael's death I prayed for Lisa, her husband Mike, and their youngest son, Matthew. I thanked God for giving me the tools to support those who need a hand.

Give It Away

It's this pay-it-forward attitude that I encourage on my website www.howtoshopforfree.net, and, to my humble amazement, my members have whole-heartedly embraced it. I continue to be touched by the incredible acts of generosity and kindness they perform toward others. When I posted a note on the site about Michael's accident, the thousands of members who extended their love and support overwhelmed me. Cards, donations, and grocery deliveries started arriving within days. Every time a Peapod grocery delivery truck pulled up, I cried. I was so moved that people would come forward to help a family they didn't even know.

SHOPPER'S
Hall of Fame

"Because most of the items I get free are toiletries I'm allergic to, I looked for a charity that could really use them. I e-mailed a local battered woman's shelter and asked if they needed my help. It was like I was offering them pure gold; they were so enthusiastic and delighted to hear from me. In just over three months, I donated over $750 worth of body wash, deodorant, shampoo, baby diapers, and formula to Refuge House. They tell me I am their 'new best friend' and treat me like royalty. It feels wonderful to not only be able to help my family, but to donate to those in need."

Regina, Tallahassee, Florida

"I've been collecting full-size body washes, deodorants, shampoos, razors, shaving cream, and all kinds of free, or almost free, things for our local firefighters. The guys who get these packages are just amazed that anyone would take the time to do this for them. I strongly encourage anyone who has extra supplies on hand to do something similar. Many of the firemen are volunteers across the country (volunteer = unpaid). These guys live at the fire stations on their days on. This means they shower, sleep, and everything else there, too. Having someone donate a few bottles of personal care items is a pretty neat thing for them. Many of our guys are single, young men who are working several jobs, and they really appreciate it."

Firefighter's wife, North Carolina

One member suggested I plant a tree in Michael's memory at the scene of the accident. I'd recently purchased a weeping willow tree (at 90 percent off) and hadn't planted it yet, so that's exactly what we did. My husband and I organized a group planting for friends and family. We planted "Michael's tree" across the street from our house and every month on the anniversary of his death, many of Michael's friends gather there to share memories of him.

They say good can come from the most horrible and unfortunate events, and I believe this is true. The loss of Michael Doherty inspired the beauty in so many to rise to the surface and radiate outward. His death has taught me to never underestimate the power of generosity.

While Michael's death invoked the spirit of giving in many individuals, it doesn't take a horrible tragedy to give you a reason to pay it forward. There are occasions to give every day of the week. Take Richard from Green Bay, Virginia, for example. Richard's a *How to Shop for Free* member who regularly gives his stockpile away because he simply can't pass up a good deal, even when he doesn't need it. Case in point: When Richard noticed an entire "sale" cart filled with boxes of spaghetti marked down to ten cents a box, he couldn't resist. He rolled the entire cart to the checkout line and bought it all. He never unloaded the spaghetti from the trunk of his car. He simply gave it away, one box at a time, to every person he encountered who looked like they might want it or could use it.

WORK IT: SPREAD THE WEALTH

Now it's your turn. Pick an individual or a local organization and make a donation of items from your stockpile. Here are a few ideas to get your wheels turning:

- Senior centers
- Community centers
- Disabled veteran programs

- Local food bank
- Meals on Wheels
- Children's shelter
- Battered women's shelter
- Homeless shelter
- Animal shelter
- Religious organizations

Many charitable organizations have "wish lists" where you can apply your shopping-for-free prowess for the greater good. Don't get hung up over how much to give. It's the simple act of giving that's most meaningful. For me, paying it forward feels better than any shopping high I've ever experienced and my guess is that once you start giving, you'll be hooked, too. Julie, a *How to Shop for Free* member calls shopping for free a "beneficial addiction." I couldn't agree more.   ✂

Shopping for free has changed my life, and I've seen it change the lives of others. My claim that clipping coupons can make the difference between financial instability and security may sound like a really bad late-night infomercial, but I'm living proof that it's true. I never worry that I won't be able to provide food, clothing, and the basic essentials for my family. In fact, my family enjoys a life of plentitude for which I'm extremely grateful. I wrote *How to Shop for Free* so that you, too, can experience more ease and less financial stress in your life. I've shared all my secrets and given you the tools so you never have to pay full price again. Now you have the power to have more of what you want for less, so get into your shopper stance, girlfriend. There's nothing stopping you now!

If you haven't already done so, subscribe to the RSS feed on www.howtoshopforfree.net and you'll receive multiple updates a day about my latest free finds in all the stores I shop (and you know I patronize a fair share). In addition, join the community forums on www.howtoshopforfree.net for the most up-to-date BOGO, Catalina, and downright killer deals to be found in most of the major grocery store and pharmacy chains. Membership is free. Better yet, you'll be joining a large and growing community of bargainistas who can help answer your most pressing coupon questions and provide you with free tips. Believe me, I learn something new from my members every day. Also, be sure to follow me on Twitter (HTSFF) for my daily Woo Hoo Deal Alerts, and find me on Facebook at How to Shop for Free where I post contests and giveaways, along with the latest, greatest printables and provide you with the links to *get* them yourself. See you online!

Acknowledgments

I wrote this book for every single mom struggling to provide for her children, and determined to do it all on her own; every married couple who feels a toll on their marriage because of financial burdens; every veteran and military employee who has defended our country and yet has a hard time providing for their own family; every senior citizen who is afraid they won't be able to afford their prescription refills, and for every generous member of How to Shop for Free who has paid it forward in one way or another.

As for acknowledgments, first and foremost, I need to thank all the community members and hard-working moderators of How to Shop for Free, www.howtoshopforfree.net. The website would not be successful without all of you. Amy, Christine, April, Lisa, Deb, Carla, Nay, Kathy, Laurie, Laura, Tina, Jen, Sherry, Lori, Jamie, Michelle, Charlene, and my alter-ego Kwim—I couldn't have done it without you. Special gratitude also goes to Anthony Scott Jr. (may he rest in peace) who inspired the HTSFF community. And also a big *Thank you, Mary* to the Coupon Fairy (she really does exist).

Thanks to Yahoo for enabling me to create a free website and Big Tent for being a huge supporter of How to Shop for Free. I always felt welcome and supported there. Mia and Rufus—you always believed in me and I am forever thankful.

Gratitude to everyone at Foundry Literary + Media Agency, especially my agent Yfat Reiss Gendell for finding me and encouraging me to write it all down and share it with the world. Thanks to my amazing writer Samantha Rose for helping me find my voice and fine-tune it. You were able to capture what I do and put it into words. Thank you for all your hard work, support, and patience.

To everyone at Da Capo Press, especially my editor Renee Sedliar. Thank you for believing in me and believing that this book would be a success. It's been an honor to work with you and to have my book published with Da Capo. Thanks also go to my fabulous publicist, Lissa Warren, editorial assistant Erica Truxler, my badass copy editor, Roberta Bell, and the folks at Eclipse Publishing Services. And I can't forget my favorite attorney Peter Smith for reviewing all my contracts for free. You're the best!

Special thanks go to the manufacturers that continue to provide me with great coupons and to all the cashiers who have rung me up and had to scan my enormous stack of coupons. You always did it with a smile on your face. And finally, I'm grateful to all my friends and family who have encouraged me to pursue this crazy coupon journey. Never underestimate the power of a coupon. They can change your life. They have, mine.

Index